THE "I LOVE MY AIR FRYER"

Affordable Meals

RECIPE BOOK

From *Meatloaf* to *Banana Bread*,
175 Delicious Meals You Can Make for under $12

Aileen Clark of AileenCooks.com
Author of The "I Love My Instant Pot®"
Affordable Meals Recipe Book

Adams Media

New York London Toronto Sydney New Delhi

For Sean. Thank you for always encouraging me to chase my dreams.

Adams Media
An Imprint of Simon & Schuster, Inc.
100 Technology Center Drive
Stoughton, Massachusetts 02072

First Adams Media trade paperback edition October 2021

ADAMS MEDIA and colophon are trademarks of Simon & Schuster.

For information about special discounts for bulk purchases, please contact Simon & Schuster Special Sales at 1-866-506-1949 or business@simonandschuster.com.

The Simon & Schuster Speakers Bureau can bring authors to your live event. For more information or to book an event contact the Simon & Schuster Speakers Bureau at 1-866-248-3049 or visit our website at www.simonspeakers.com.

Photographs by James Stefiuk

Manufactured in the United States of America

2 2022

Library of Congress Cataloging-in-Publication Data
Names: Clark, Aileen, author.
Title: The "I love my air fryer" affordable meals recipe book / Aileen Clark of AileenCooks.com, Author of The "I Love My Instant Pot®" Affordable Meals Recipe Book.
Description: Stoughton, Massachusetts: Adams Media, 2021. | Series: "I love my" series | Includes index.
Identifiers: LCCN 2021021474 | ISBN 9781507215791 (pb) | ISBN 9781507215807 (ebook)
Subjects: LCSH: Hot air frying. | LCGFT: Cookbooks.
Classification: LCC TX689 .C58 2021 | DDC 641.7/7--dc23
LC record available at https://lccn.loc.gov/2021021474

ISBN 978-1-5072-1579-1
ISBN 978-1-5072-1580-7 (ebook)

Contents

Introduction

Cooking delicious and nutritious foods does not have to cost a fortune. While the term "affordable food" may conjure up the idea of food that is bland, overly processed, and unhealthy, the truth is you can cook foods that are wholesome and tasty and save money at the same time.

That is where the air fryer comes in! This multifunctional kitchen tool can take the place of other appliances in your kitchen like your oven, microwave, deep fryer, and dehydrator *and* cook delicious meals in a fraction of the time you're used to. You can use your air fryer to prepare nearly every meal, from breakfast and side dishes to dinner and dessert.

Air fryer cooking can also save you money. Not only does it make meal preparation fast and tasty, but it helps re-create those pricey restaurant-style meals you love at home for a fraction of the cost! This cookbook will give you the recipes and tips you need to make affordable and tasty meals that cost $12 or less.

This air fryer cookbook is designed for both the beginner air fryer user and the experienced air fryer user. You will learn how to make new and exciting dishes in your air fryer, as well as how to choose the best air fryer for your needs, which accessories to invest in, and how to deal with cook time variations. Then you'll dig into delicious recipes like zesty Chicken Taquitos, savory Brown Sugar Pork Chops, sweet Honey Garlic Salmon, and flaky and warm Pull-Apart Dinner Rolls.

This cookbook will offer many ways to create yummy recipes with affordable ingredients. Inside you will find 175 recipes that range from Denver-Style Frittata and Blue Cheese Burgers to Crab Cakes and Bacon-Wrapped Chicken. For your sweet tooth, there is also an entire dessert chapter where you'll learn how to make Peanut Butter Cookies, Peach Hand Pies, Chocolate Chunk Brownies, and so much more!

The "I Love My Air Fryer" Affordable Meals Recipe Book will be the only cookbook you need to make your air fryer your new favorite kitchen appliance! So bring this cookbook into your kitchen and get cooking.

Cooking with an Air Fryer

Cooking with an air fryer may seem daunting at first, but it is actually incredibly easy! Not only does it make tasty fried foods without all of the oil; it can also cook everything from breakfast to dessert in almost no time. Air-fried food comes out tasting amazing because the air fryer technology adds an extra crispness that you used to only be able to get with a deep fryer.

In this chapter, you will learn the basics of cooking with an air fryer, how to choose an air fryer, and how to learn to use your particular model. You will also get practical tips on saving money on groceries along with how the cost of each recipe is calculated.

Air Fryer Basics

An air fryer is a great alternative to deep-frying food. It is a healthier option, and foods come out crispier than they would in the microwave or even in the oven. Air fryers not only make traditional deep-fried food, but they can also cook chicken and steak, fry vegetables to a perfect crisp, serve up breakfast items such as bacon, and make lots of fun desserts like cookies and hand pies.

Air fryers also don't heat up your kitchen the way a traditional oven does. They are a great way to cook in the summer without adding extra heat to your home. Air fryers also tend to cook things quite quickly. Many recipes take 30 minutes or less to cook, and several take 10 minutes or less to cook. In addition, air fryers take up very little space in your kitchen compared to other appliances and can even be taken with you to parties, to potlucks, and on vacations.

Choosing an Air Fryer

There are two different types of air fryers (and many, many different brands). The two main types of air fryers are basket-style and oven style. Either is a great option, and which you choose depends on your personal preferences. Also, either kind of air fryer can be used when making the recipes in this cookbook.

- **Basket-style** air fryers take up less space on your counter and can be easier to clean.
- **Oven-style** air fryers tend to have extra options, like rotisserie, but are more difficult to clean. Oven-style air fryers also hold more food, making it less likely that you will need to cook recipes in batches, as you may need to with a basket-style air fryer.

Another thing to look for when purchasing an air fryer is the capacity inside the air fryer. You should look for one that is at least 5 quarts. Even if you are cooking for only one or two people, you will run into times when you will want enough room to cook more than one serving, and the extra food may not fit inside a smaller air fryer.

Many air fryers offer additional capabilities. Some can also work as dehydrators, roasters, and rotisseries. Make a list of the capabilities you want before shopping for an air fryer so you can ensure you get the one with all of the bells and whistles you wish for.

Air Fryer Accessories

You don't need a lot of accessories for your air fryer, but there are a few mentioned in this book that you may want to purchase:

- **Small cake pan:** This pan is used for cakes, quiches, and casseroles. The cake pan used in this cookbook is a 7" cake pan. Make sure the pan you get fits inside of your selected air fryer.
- **Silicone egg mold:** This is perfect for eggs and muffins.
- **Small Bundt pan:** Bundt pans make recipes look pretty and are great for making pull-apart recipes like pizza bread and monkey bread.

Safe Removal of Accessories

When removing accessories and food from an air fryer, you should treat them as if you were using an oven. Everything inside the air fryer gets very hot and will burn you if you are not careful. Make sure to take extra precautions by always using oven mitts when removing food and accessories from your air fryer. Tongs are also a great tool to have on hand for flipping foods over and removing them from your air fryer.

Cook Time Variations

As there are many different variations of air fryers, there are cook time variations too. Whenever you're trying a new recipe, keep an eye on your food, as it may need to be taken out of the air fryer a couple of minutes early or air fried for a couple of extra minutes. This is normal. As you get used to your air fryer, you will learn how quickly it cooks. It also helps to add a note in the cookbook if you ended up needing to change the air fry time.

Preheating an Air Fryer

All of the recipes in this cookbook require the air fryer to be preheated prior to cooking. This offers a consistency and helps keep the cooking times accurate. Refer to your air fryer owner's manual on directions for preheating your air fryer.

Using Cooking Spray

In this cookbook, you will see that only olive oil spray is recommended to spray inside your air fryer. Standard nonstick sprays contain additional chemicals that can wear down the coating in your air fryer. Make sure to read the ingredients when purchasing the olive oil spray to ensure it contains only oil.

Cleaning Your Air Fryer

It's important to clean your air fryer after each use. Don't wait to clean your air fryer or the food will get caked on and will be much harder to wash. First, make sure your air fryer is unplugged and cooled down. Start by washing your air fryer basket or trays with warm, soapy water. Use a toothpick or other small, sharp tool to clean out any food stuck in the air holes. Wipe the inside of the air fryer with a damp towel. Finally, wipe the outside of the air fryer with a damp towel.

How to Save Money on Groceries

You probably purchased this air fryer cookbook because you want to save money on groceries while still making delicious food. Well, you are in the right place! This book is filled with recipes that use inexpensive ingredients to make delicious and filling meals. There are also two main rules for saving money on groceries I want you to focus on when using this cookbook: planning your meals and not wasting ingredients.

Plan Your Meals

The best way to plan your meals is to take an inventory of your pantry and plan your meals around the ingredients you already have on hand. Plan out what you will cook for each meal for the entire week—leaving a day here or there to eat up any leftovers you may have or for unexpected nights out. Be sure to write down your meal plan. If it is not in writing, you will likely forget or not stick with the plan.

Once you have an inventory of your current pantry and refrigerator items, make a grocery list of the additional items you need to make your meals. This will prevent you from being left with three half-used bags of rice and inspire you to use up the rest of the pasta you bought last month and forgot about. If you do find multiple packages of the same item in your kitchen, use the one that is set to expire first.

Another great way to save money while planning your meals is checking the weekly grocery flyers to see which items are on sale. You will get the most bang for your buck by planning around the meat and produce sales. Simply figure out which items are on sale and plan your dinners around those items and the items you already have on hand. Taking the time to do this can save you a lot of money.

Also, make sure you are purchasing meat and produce items your family actually likes to eat. It won't save you any money if you don't end up using it!

If possible, try ordering your groceries online and picking them up at the store. Many retailers now offer this service, and it can save a lot of money on impulse purchases. If you are not walking around the store, then you are less likely to buy something extra on impulse.

Use Coupons

If you do end up shopping in a store, make sure you check a coupon app for the items on your list. There are many coupon apps out there that allow you to select rebates on popular coupon items and scan your receipt after purchase. Once you reach a certain threshold (anywhere from $5–$20), the app will send you a check. Use that money toward future grocery purchases. Some great apps for cash back on groceries are Ibotta and Checkout 51.

If you want to use actual coupons in the store, try Coupon Sherpa or Coupons.com. Both of these apps show coupons available for in-store savings. Coupon Sherpa allows coupons to be scanned directly from your smartphone, and Coupons.com lets you link the coupons to your store's loyalty card.

Buy in Bulk

Purchasing in bulk is another great way to save money, if done right. Start by making a list of the ingredients you use every single week and purchase regularly. For example, for many people, that might be meat like ground beef. Next, determine if you have extra room to store bulk items—pantry space for dry goods or freezer space for meat. Lastly, check your local grocery store prices on the same item before buying in bulk (many grocery stores will show you prices online).

Not all bulk purchases are a better deal, so it's important to check before heading to your local bulk store. If you can check off all three of these steps, then set some money aside to buy in bulk. It will save you money in the long run.

Don't Waste Ingredients

Now comes the fun part—the cooking! Being a frugal cook takes some practice. The hardest part for many people is actually making what you planned and not wasting those ingredients. A great way to ensure this happens is by pulling out all of the nonperishable items you need for that day's recipe and leaving them on your counter in the morning (or even the night before). It's a great visual reminder to get cooking and not waste the food you purchased.

Another helpful tool is a magnetic dry-erase board with the week's meal plan hanging on your refrigerator. That way you will see it every time you open your refrigerator.

If at the end of the week you find yourself with leftover ingredients, I challenge you to get creative and use them up. Don't let them go to waste. You can try repurposing them into a new meal or simply freezing any items that can be stored in the freezer until you can use them. Most things can be frozen if packaged properly. Just make sure you create a label for it (wet erase markers are perfect for this), so you don't forget what it is you froze. Then add those ingredients to your inventory for the next week's meal plan.

How the Recipe Costs Are Calculated

You will see that every recipe in this cookbook has a cost included. The recipes are calculated by the portion of ingredients used (e.g., 1 teaspoon dried parsley), not the entire package. The recipe costs are based on a national food retailer's prices and are accurate at the time of publication.

2

Breakfast

Making breakfast in the air fryer is a wonderful way to be better about eating breakfast in the morning—even if you don't have a lot of time to spend in the kitchen. Many of the recipes in this chapter can be used to make your breakfast ahead of time so you can grab and go or quickly reheat the breakfast in the air fryer before leaving for the day. This chapter also includes recipes for those slower days when you have more time to make a fresh and tasty breakfast. In this chapter, you'll find recipes like Bacon Egg Bites, Mushroom and Swiss Frittata, Brioche French Toast, and Strawberry Breakfast Pastries.

Crispy Bacon

Bacon in an air fryer comes out perfectly crisp around the edges with a chewy center. Air frying bacon can sometimes cause smoke to come out of the air fryer. To help prevent this, add ¼ cup of water to the bottom of your air fryer before cooking the bacon. Store any uneaten bacon in an airtight container in the refrigerator up to 3 days.

Hands-On Time: 5 minutes
Cook Time: 10 minutes
Total Recipe Cost: $2.52

Serves 6

6 slices bacon

1 Preheat air fryer to 320°F. Line a plate with paper towels.

2 Arrange bacon in an even layer inside air fryer. Air fry 5 minutes.

3 Use tongs to carefully flip bacon over.

4 Air fry an additional 5 minutes until crispy.

5 Place bacon on prepared plate to absorb any excess grease. Serve.

PER SERVING

CALORIES: 43 | **FAT:** 3g | **PROTEIN:** 4g | **SODIUM:** 162mg | **FIBER:** 0g | **CARBOHYDRATES:** 0g | **SUGAR:** 0g

Breakfast Sausage Links

You will love cooking breakfast sausages in an air fryer because they stay incredibly juicy while having an extra-crispy texture around the outside. Air-fried breakfast sausages are perfect for mixing into a burrito or omelet or eating on their own. Store any uneaten sausage links in an airtight container in the refrigerator up to 4 days.

Hands-On Time: 5 minutes
Cook Time: 10 minutes
Total Recipe Cost: $1.65

Serves 4

8 ounces pork breakfast sausage links

WHAT ABOUT SAUSAGE PATTIES?

Breakfast sausage patties can be cooked using the same method. Add 1-2 minutes of air frying time for larger sausage patties and keep the cook time to 10 minutes for smaller sausage patties.

1 Preheat air fryer to 390°F.

2 Arrange sausage links in an even layer inside air fryer.

3 Air fry 10 minutes, flipping halfway through the cooking time.

4 Serve immediately.

PER SERVING

CALORIES: 149 | FAT: 12g | PROTEIN: 9g | SODIUM: 374mg | FIBER: 0g | CARBOHYDRATES: 1g | SUGAR: 1g

Mushroom and Swiss Frittata

If you love a good frittata, then making it in the air fryer is for you. This sophisticated combination of mushrooms, Swiss, and baby spinach tastes like it was made in a restaurant, yet it costs way less when prepared at home. Leftover frittata can be stored in an airtight container in the refrigerator up to 3 days.

Hands-On Time: 10 minutes
Cook Time: 12 minutes
Total Recipe Cost: $3.49

Serves 4

4 large eggs
½ cup whole milk
¾ cup shredded Swiss cheese, divided
½ cup diced cremini mushrooms
¼ cup chopped baby spinach
1 teaspoon minced garlic
½ teaspoon salt
¼ teaspoon ground black pepper

1 Preheat air fryer to 360°F. Grease a 7" cake pan and set aside.

2 In a medium bowl, whisk together eggs. Then add milk, ½ cup cheese, mushrooms, spinach, garlic, salt, and pepper and whisk again to combine. Pour egg mixture into prepared cake pan.

3 Place pan inside air fryer. Air fry 11 minutes.

4 Sprinkle top of frittata with remaining ¼ cup cheese and air fry an additional 1 minute until cheese is melted.

5 Let pan sit 5 minutes before serving.

PER SERVING

CALORIES: 170 | FAT: 11g | PROTEIN: 13g | SODIUM: 390mg | FIBER: 0g | CARBOHYDRATES: 4g | SUGAR: 2g

Hard-Cooked Eggs

No, you don't have to make these Hard-Cooked Eggs in boiling water! You can cook them quickly and easily in an air fryer. They are ready in just 20 minutes. Be sure to follow the directions at the end for chilling them in an ice bath, as this helps the shell peel away easily.

Hands-On Time: 5 minutes
Cook Time: 15 minutes
Total Recipe Cost: $0.82

Serves 6

6 large eggs
4 cups water
2 cups ice

HOW LONG WILL THE EGGS LAST?

If stored properly, Hard-Cooked Eggs will stay fresh in the refrigerator for 1 week. It's important to refrigerate them within 2 hours of cooking. They should be stored with the shell on and in an airtight container.

1 Preheat air fryer to 270°F.

2 Arrange eggs in a single layer inside air fryer. Air fry 15 minutes.

3 In a large bowl, combine water and ice.

4 Place eggs in bowl of ice water. Let sit 10 minutes.

5 Remove eggs from ice bath and peel under cold running water. Serve immediately.

PER SERVING

CALORIES: 77 | FAT: 4g | PROTEIN: 6g | SODIUM: 62mg | FIBER: 0g | CARBOHYDRATES: 1g | SUGAR: 1g

Denver-Style Frittata

Different vegetables may be substituted in this recipe. The most important part is to ensure the vegetables are diced into small pieces, so they cook thoroughly in the air fryer. If you're adding a harder vegetable like sweet potato, it will need to be cooked ahead of time before you add it to the frittata to be cooked in the air fryer. Leftover frittata can be stored in an airtight container in the refrigerator up to 3 days.

Hands-On Time: 10 minutes
Cook Time: 12 minutes
Total Recipe Cost: $2.75

Serves 4

4 large eggs
½ cup whole milk
½ cup diced ham
½ cup shredded sharp
    Cheddar cheese, divided
¼ cup diced green bell
    pepper
¼ cup diced white onion
½ teaspoon salt
¼ teaspoon ground black
    pepper

1   Preheat air fryer to 360°F. Grease a 7" cake pan and set aside.

2   In a medium bowl, whisk together eggs. Then add milk, ham, ¼ cup cheese, bell pepper, onion, salt, and black pepper and whisk again to combine. Pour egg mixture into prepared cake pan.

3   Carefully place pan inside air fryer. Air fry 11 minutes.

4   Sprinkle top of frittata with remaining ¼ cup cheese. Air fry an additional 1 minute until cheese is melted.

5   Let pan sit 5 minutes before serving.

PER SERVING

CALORIES: 182 | FAT: 11g | PROTEIN: 15g | SODIUM: 708mg | FIBER: 1g | CARBOHYDRATES: 4g | SUGAR: 2g

Bacon Egg Bites

If you love buying those egg bites from your local coffee shop, then you are going to love this recipe. Bacon Egg Bites can be made in bulk and enjoyed all week as a quick and easy breakfast. Simply reheat them in the microwave 30–45 seconds and then enjoy. Uneaten egg bites can be stored in an airtight container in the refrigerator up to 5 days.

Hands-On Time: 10 minutes
Cook Time: 17 minutes
Total Recipe Cost: $4.13

Serves 6

6 large eggs
¾ cup whole milk
1 cup crumbled cooked bacon
¾ cup shredded sharp Cheddar cheese, divided
½ teaspoon salt
¼ teaspoon ground black pepper

1 Preheat air fryer to 300°F. Grease a six-hole silicone egg mold and set aside.

2 In a medium bowl, whisk together eggs. Then add milk, bacon, ½ cup cheese, salt, and pepper and whisk again to combine.

3 Pour egg mixture into prepared egg mold and carefully place egg mold inside air fryer.

4 Air fry 16 minutes until egg mixture is no longer jiggly, then sprinkle egg bites with remaining ¼ cup cheese.

5 Air fry an additional 1 minute until cheese is melted. Serve immediately.

PER SERVING

CALORIES: 263 | **FAT:** 17g | **PROTEIN:** 20g | **SODIUM:** 801mg | **FIBER:** 0g | **CARBOHYDRATES:** 2g | **SUGAR:** 2g

Vegetable Egg Bites

These egg bites are perfect if you are vegetarian or are trying to add more vegetables into your diet. You can also use any vegetables you have on hand to make this recipe. Be sure to dice whatever vegetables you choose into small pieces. Store any uneaten egg bites in an airtight container in the refrigerator up to 3 days.

Hands-On Time: 10 minutes
Cook Time: 17 minutes
Total Recipe Cost: $2.76

Serves 6

6 large eggs
¾ cup whole milk
½ cup shredded mozzarella cheese, divided
2 tablespoons chopped baby spinach
2 tablespoons diced green bell pepper
2 tablespoons diced red bell pepper
2 tablespoons diced white mushrooms
½ teaspoon salt
¼ teaspoon ground black pepper

1 Preheat air fryer to 300°F. Grease a six-hole silicone egg mold and set aside.

2 In a medium bowl, whisk together eggs. Then add milk, ¼ cup cheese, spinach, green bell pepper, red bell pepper, mushrooms, salt, and black pepper and whisk again to combine.

3 Pour egg mixture into prepared egg mold and carefully place egg mold inside air fryer.

4 Air fry 16 minutes until egg mixture is no longer jiggly, then sprinkle with remaining ¼ cup cheese.

5 Air fry an additional 1 minute until cheese is melted. Serve immediately.

PER SERVING

CALORIES: 119 | FAT: 7g | PROTEIN: 9g | SODIUM: 336mg | FIBER: 0g | CARBOHYDRATES: 2g | SUGAR: 2g

Puffed Egg Tarts

These fancy egg tarts are the perfect addition to your brunch table! Be careful when adding the eggs to the puff pastry, as they have a tendency to slip off.

Hands-On Time: 15 minutes
Cook Time: 15 minutes
Total Recipe Cost: $4.78

Serves 4

- 1 sheet frozen puff pastry, thawed
- ½ cup shredded sharp Cheddar cheese
- 4 large eggs
- 4 medium cherry tomatoes, halved
- ½ teaspoon salt
- ¼ teaspoon ground black pepper

1 Preheat air fryer to 325°F.

2 Roll out puff pastry and cut into four equal squares.

3 Fold over edges of pastry squares to create a crust. Prick center of each pastry square with a fork.

4 Spray inside of air fryer with olive oil spray. Place pastry squares inside air fryer and air fry 8 minutes just until puffed up and light golden brown.

5 Remove pastry squares from air fryer and let cool slightly, about 2 minutes.

6 Press down on the center of each pastry square with the back side of a spoon to deflate.

7 Sprinkle the center of each pastry square with cheese.

8 Crack an egg into the center of each pastry, being careful to not let it slide off the pastry square.

9 Arrange 2 tomato halves around the egg yolk of each pastry and sprinkle with salt and pepper.

10 Place pastry squares back inside air fryer and air fry 7 minutes until eggs are set. For best results, serve immediately.

PER SERVING

CALORIES: 473 | FAT: 31g | PROTEIN: 14g | SODIUM: 607mg | FIBER: 1g | CARBOHYDRATES: 29g | SUGAR: 1g

Sausage Breakfast Burritos

Breakfast burritos are a great option for making breakfast for several days at once. You'll love cooking burritos in an air fryer because they make the tortilla perfectly crispy. Store any uneaten burritos in an airtight container in the refrigerator up to 3 days.

Hands-On Time: 10 minutes
Cook Time: 3 minutes
Total Recipe Cost: $5.06

Serves 4

6 large eggs, cooked scrambled

8 ounces cooked and chopped breakfast sausage

1 cup shredded sharp Cheddar cheese

½ teaspoon salt

¼ teaspoon ground black pepper

4 (10") flour tortillas

1 Preheat air fryer to 390°F.

2 In a medium bowl, combine eggs, sausage, cheese, salt, and pepper. Gently stir.

3 Scoop even amounts of egg mixture into the center of each tortilla. Roll each tortilla into a burrito.

4 Spray inside of air fryer with olive oil spray.

5 Place burritos inside air fryer in a single layer with ½" between each burrito.

6 Spray burritos with olive oil spray and air fry 3 minutes until crispy. Serve immediately.

PER SERVING

CALORIES: 645 | FAT: 38g | PROTEIN: 30g | SODIUM: 1,548mg | FIBER: 2g | CARBOHYDRATES: 38g | SUGAR: 3g

Breakfast Quesadillas

Be careful to secure your quesadillas with toothpicks so the tortilla tops don't blow off while air frying. Store any uneaten quesadillas in an airtight container in the refrigerator up to 3 days.

Hands-On Time: 10 minutes
Cook Time: 3 minutes (per batch)
Total Recipe Cost: $4.21

Serves 4

- 4 large eggs, cooked scrambled
- 1 cup shredded Mexican cheese blend
- ½ (4-ounce) can diced mild green chilies, drained
- ½ teaspoon salt
- ¼ teaspoon ground black pepper
- 4 (10") flour tortillas

1 Preheat air fryer to 390°F.

2 In a medium bowl, combine eggs, cheese, green chilies, salt, and pepper. Stir gently.

3 Scoop even amounts of egg mixture onto one side of each tortilla. Fold over tortillas so each tortilla is a half circle and secure each with three toothpicks.

4 Spray inside of air fryer with olive oil spray.

5 Working in batches, spray quesadillas with olive oil spray and carefully place inside air fryer.

6 Air fry 3 minutes until crispy, flipping halfway through the cooking time. Serve immediately.

PER SERVING

CALORIES: 390 | FAT: 16g | PROTEIN: 19g | SODIUM: 1,060mg | FIBER: 3g | CARBOHYDRATES: 40g | SUGAR: 4g

Brioche French Toast

When I make French toast, brioche bread is my go-to favorite. Its light and fluffy texture soaks up the egg well, creating a crispy outside and custard-like center. Store any uneaten French toast in an airtight container in the refrigerator up to 3 days.

Hands-On Time: 15 minutes
Cook Time: 8 minutes (per batch)
Total Recipe Cost: $4.03

Serves 4

6 large eggs
½ cup half-and-half
1 teaspoon ground cinnamon
1 teaspoon vanilla extract
½ teaspoon salt
8 (1") slices brioche bread

WHAT ABOUT DIFFERENT BREAD?

Brioche is used in this recipe to give you that restaurant-quality flavor while saving you money by cooking at home. However, you can use any bread you have on hand in this French toast recipe. Whole-wheat bread, sourdough, and even hot dog buns work well for homemade French toast.

1 Preheat air fryer to 350°F.

2 In a medium shallow bowl, whisk together eggs, half-and-half, cinnamon, vanilla, and salt.

3 Dip each bread slice into egg mixture, turning to coat. Shake any excess moisture off the bread and set aside on a plate.

4 Spray inside of air fryer with olive oil. Working in batches, arrange bread slices inside air fryer, spaced ½" apart.

5 Air fry 8 minutes, flipping halfway through the cooking time, until golden brown. Serve immediately.

PER SERVING

CALORIES: 315 | FAT: 12g | PROTEIN: 15g | SODIUM: 692mg | FIBER: 0g | CARBOHYDRATES: 34g | SUGAR: 6g

Cinnamon French Toast Sticks

French toast sticks are a fun way to enjoy French toast. Make sure to let the excess egg mixture drip off the slices before air frying. Otherwise, the extra egg will drip through to the bottom of the air fryer and go to waste. Store any uneaten French toast sticks in an airtight container in the refrigerator and eat within 3 days.

Hands-On Time: 15 minutes
Cook Time: 6 minutes
Total Recipe Cost: $2.47

Serves 4

4 large eggs
¼ cup half-and-half
1 tablespoon ground cinnamon
1 tablespoon packed light brown sugar
1 teaspoon vanilla extract
¼ teaspoon ground nutmeg
¼ teaspoon salt
⅛ teaspoon ground cloves
4 slices country-style white bread, cut into 1" strips

1 Preheat air fryer to 350°F.

2 In a medium shallow bowl, whisk together eggs, half-and-half, cinnamon, brown sugar, vanilla, nutmeg, salt, and cloves.

3 Dip a strip of bread in egg mixture, turning to coat. Remove bread and let any excess egg mixture drip off before placing on a plate.

4 Repeat with remaining bread strips and stack them all on a plate.

5 Spray inside of air fryer with olive oil spray. Arrange French toast sticks in an even layer inside air fryer.

6 Air fry 6 minutes, flipping halfway through the cooking time. Serve immediately.

PER SERVING

CALORIES: 185 | **FAT:** 5g | **PROTEIN:** 9g | **SODIUM:** 388mg | **FIBER:** 2g | **CARBOHYDRATES:** 23g | **SUGAR:** 6g

Strawberry Breakfast Pastries

Make your own crispy and sweet breakfast pastries at home with just a handful of ingredients. This recipe uses premade pie crusts to save time in the morning. Store any uneaten pastries in an airtight container at room temperature up to 3 days.

Hands-On Time: 15 minutes
Cook Time: 8 minutes (per batch)
Total Recipe Cost: $3.52

Serves 5

2 (9") premade pie crusts
1 cup strawberry jam
1 large egg
1 tablespoon water
½ cup vanilla icing
¼ cup rainbow sprinkles

1 Preheat air fryer to 375°F.

2 Roll out pie crusts and cut out ten 3" rectangles. Divide rectangles in half.

3 Place 1 tablespoon jam in the center of half of the rectangles.

4 Place remaining rectangles on top of jam-filled ones. Press edges together with the tines of a fork.

5 In a small bowl, whisk together egg and water to make an egg wash. Brush egg wash on top of each pastry.

6 Place pastries inside air fryer, spaced ½" apart (you may need to work in batches).

7 Air fry 8 minutes just until pastries start to get golden brown around the edges. Make sure to check them often, as they can burn quickly.

8 Spread icing on top of pastries, then top with sprinkles. Serve warm.

PER SERVING

CALORIES: 745 | FAT: 28g | PROTEIN: 4g | SODIUM: 457mg | FIBER: 2g | CARBOHYDRATES: 118g | SUGAR: 57g

Banana Bread

I love air fryer Banana Bread because it makes delicious small batches quick and easy! Make two small loaves of perfectly moist Banana Bread with the perfect crispy crust with this recipe. Uneaten bread can be wrapped in plastic wrap and stored in an airtight container at room temperature up to 3 days.

Hands-On Time: 10 minutes
Cook Time: 28 minutes
Total Recipe Cost: $1.02

Serves 4

- 1 large ripe banana, peeled and mashed
- ¾ cup all-purpose flour
- 1 large egg
- 3 tablespoons packed light brown sugar
- 2 tablespoons unsalted butter, melted and cooled slightly
- ¼ cup sour cream
- ½ teaspoon baking soda
- ¼ teaspoon salt

1 Preheat air fryer to 320°F. Grease two mini loaf pans and set aside.

2 In a medium bowl, combine all ingredients. Stir until evenly combined.

3 Evenly divide batter between prepared pans.

4 Air fry 28 minutes until golden brown on top and a toothpick inserted in the center of bread comes out clean.

5 Let cool 30 minutes before serving.

PER SERVING

CALORIES: 250 | FAT: 9g | PROTEIN: 5g | SODIUM: 331mg | FIBER: 2g | CARBOHYDRATES: 36g | SUGAR: 15g

Chocolate Chip Banana Muffins

Muffins come out extra brown on top in the air fryer, but they still have the perfect crumb texture in the center. Chocolate Chip Banana Muffins bring the perfect moisture and flavor from the banana and that extra bite of sweetness—thanks to the mini chocolate chips. Store any uneaten muffins in an airtight container at room temperature up to 3 days.

Hands-On Time: 15 minutes
Cook Time: 14 minutes
Total Recipe Cost: $1.83

Serves 6

1 cup all-purpose flour
½ cup granulated sugar
1 large egg
¼ cup buttermilk
⅛ cup plain Greek yogurt
3 tablespoons unsalted
    butter, melted
½ teaspoon vanilla extract
½ teaspoon baking powder
¼ teaspoon baking soda
¼ teaspoon salt
1 large ripe banana, peeled
    and mashed
½ cup mini chocolate chips

1 Preheat air fryer to 320°F. Grease a six-hole silicone egg mold and set aside.

2 In a medium bowl, mix together flour, sugar, egg, buttermilk, yogurt, melted butter, vanilla, baking powder, baking soda, and salt. Stir until no longer dry but still lumpy.

3 Fold in mashed banana and chocolate ships. Stir just until evenly distributed.

4 Scoop banana mixture into prepared egg mold. Carefully place egg mold inside air fryer.

5 Air fry 14 minutes until a toothpick inserted in the center of a muffin comes out clean. Serve immediately.

PER SERVING

CALORIES: 309 | FAT: 10g | PROTEIN: 5g | SODIUM: 226mg |
FIBER: 2g | CARBOHYDRATES: 47g | SUGAR: 27g

Blueberry Muffins

A good blueberry muffin can be hard to come by, but these fit the bill! They are moist, with just the right amount of sweetness. Raspberries can be used in place of blueberries in this recipe if desired. Store any uneaten muffins in an airtight container at room temperature up to 3 days.

Hands-On Time: 15 minutes
Cook Time: 15 minutes
Total Recipe Cost: $2.69

Serves 6

1 cup all-purpose flour
½ cup granulated sugar
1 large egg
¼ cup buttermilk
6 tablespoons unsalted butter, melted
½ teaspoon vanilla extract
1¼ teaspoons baking powder
¾ teaspoon ground cinnamon
⅛ teaspoon ground nutmeg
¼ teaspoon salt
1 cup blueberries

1 Preheat air fryer to 350°F. Grease a six-hole silicone egg mold and set aside.

2 In a medium bowl, mix together flour, sugar, egg, buttermilk, melted butter, vanilla, baking powder, cinnamon, nutmeg, and salt. Stir until no longer dry but still lumpy.

3 Fold in blueberries. Stir just until evenly distributed.

4 Scoop mixture into prepared egg mold, filling each hole ¾ full. Carefully place egg mold inside air fryer.

5 Air fry 15 minutes until a toothpick inserted in the center of a muffin comes out clean. Serve immediately.

PER SERVING

CALORIES: 275 | FAT: 12g | PROTEIN: 4g | SODIUM: 223mg | FIBER: 1g | CARBOHYDRATES: 37g | SUGAR: 20g

Coffee Cake

Coffee Cake is the perfect pairing for a leisurely morning over tea or coffee. The best part is this recipe is ready in under an hour! Don't skip the sour cream, as it is very important for making the perfect texture. Wrap any uneaten Coffee Cake in plastic wrap and store in an airtight container in the refrigerator up to 1 week.

Hands-On Time: 20 minutes
Cook Time: 30 minutes
Total Recipe Cost: $2.54

Serves 6

2½ cups all-purpose flour, divided
¾ cup granulated sugar, divided
½ cup packed light brown sugar, divided
2 teaspoons baking powder
¾ teaspoon salt, divided
1 large egg
¾ cup sour cream
¾ cup unsalted butter, melted and divided
1½ teaspoons vanilla extract, divided
1 teaspoon ground cinnamon
½ cup confectioners' sugar
1 tablespoon whole milk

1 Preheat air fryer to 320°F. Grease a 7" cake pan and set aside.

2 In a large bowl, whisk together 2 cups flour, ½ cup granulated sugar, ¼ cup brown sugar, baking powder, and ½ teaspoon salt.

3 Make a well in the center of the dry ingredients and add egg, sour cream, ½ cup melted butter, and 1 teaspoon vanilla. Stir until batter is well combined.

4 In a medium bowl, combine remaining ½ cup flour, remaining ¼ cup granulated sugar, remaining ¼ cup brown sugar, remaining ¼ teaspoon salt, remaining ¼ cup melted butter, and cinnamon. Mix with a fork until a streusel with pea-sized crumbs is formed.

5 Pour half of batter into prepared cake pan. Top with half of streusel. Repeat with remaining batter and streusel.

6 Place cake pan inside air fryer. Air fry 30 minutes until a toothpick inserted in the center of cake comes out clean. Let cake cool on a cooling rack 30 minutes.

7 Once Coffee Cake is cooled, whisk together remaining ½ teaspoon vanilla, confectioners' sugar, and milk. Drizzle icing over cake and serve.

PER SERVING

CALORIES: 665 | FAT: 28g | PROTEIN: 7g | SODIUM: 488mg | FIBER: 2g | CARBOHYDRATES: 93g | SUGAR: 52g

Glazed Doughnuts

Make your own doughnuts at home using canned biscuits and a tasty homemade vanilla glaze! You can find canned biscuits in the refrigerated section of your grocery store. These doughnuts are best eaten on the same day you make them.

Hands-On Time: 10 minutes
Cook Time: 6 minutes
Total Recipe Cost: $3.42

Serves 8

1 (16.3-ounce) can refrigerated biscuit dough
3 cups confectioners' sugar
¼ cup whole milk
¼ cup unsalted butter, melted
1 teaspoon vanilla extract

WANT CHOCOLATE GLAZE FOR YOUR DOUGHNUTS?

If you want to make a chocolate glaze, combine ½ cup semisweet chocolate chips, 3 tablespoons heavy cream, and 2 tablespoons unsalted butter in a medium microwave-safe bowl. Microwave in 30-second increments, stirring each time, until melted. Stir until smooth and shiny. Dip the top of each doughnut in the chocolate glaze and let sit an additional 5 minutes before serving.

1 Preheat air fryer to 360°F. Spray inside air fryer with olive oil spray.

2 Remove dough from can and separate into eight biscuits. Using a small cookie cutter or shot glass, cut a hole out in the center of each biscuit to make a doughnut shape. Discard remaining biscuit dough or save for another day.

3 Place doughnuts inside air fryer, spaced ½" apart, and air fry 6 minutes, flipping halfway through the cooking time.

4 While doughnuts are cooking, make vanilla glaze in a medium bowl by whisking together confectioners' sugar, milk, melted butter, and vanilla until creamy.

5 Use tongs to remove doughnuts from air fryer and dip in glaze. Flip to fully coat the doughnuts in glaze.

6 Place doughnuts on a cooling rack. Let sit 5 minutes before serving.

PER SERVING

CALORIES: 371 | **FAT:** 11g | **PROTEIN:** 4g | **SODIUM:** 526mg | **FIBER:** 1g | **CARBOHYDRATES:** 63g | **SUGAR:** 41g

Monkey Bread

Monkey Bread is a cross between a coffee cake and a cinnamon roll. Bits of dough are coated in cinnamon and sugar before being arranged in a Bundt pan. Then they are drizzled in melted butter and brown sugar and air fried to gooey perfection. Store any uneaten portions in an airtight container at room temperature and enjoy within 1 day.

Hands-On Time: 20 minutes
Cook Time: 12 minutes
Total Recipe Cost: $3.34

Serves 6

- 1 (16.3-ounce) can refrigerated biscuit dough
- 1 cup granulated sugar
- 3 tablespoons ground cinnamon
- ½ cup packed light brown sugar
- ½ cup unsalted butter
- ½ teaspoon vanilla extract

1 Preheat air fryer to 320°F. Grease a small Bundt pan and set aside.

2 Remove dough from can and cut each round into 1" pieces.

3 In a large zip-top plastic bag, combine dough pieces, granulated sugar, and cinnamon. Close bag and shake until dough pieces are evenly coated with sugar and cinnamon.

4 Remove dough pieces from bag and arrange in prepared Bundt pan.

5 In a small saucepan over medium heat, combine brown sugar and butter until butter is melted and sugar is dissolved, about 2 minutes.

6 Whisk in vanilla and turn off heat.

7 Pour butter mixture over dough pieces and place Bundt pan inside air fryer.

8 Air fry 10 minutes until golden brown. Serve immediately.

PER SERVING

CALORIES: 594 | **FAT:** 22g | **PROTEIN:** 6g | **SODIUM:** 779mg | **FIBER:** 4g | **CARBOHYDRATES:** 92g | **SUGAR:** 58g

Homemade Hash Browns

Homemade Hash Browns come out tasting so fresh and crispy! Make sure to squeeze as much moisture out of the shredded potatoes as possible prior to cooking. These cooked hash browns can be stored in the refrigerator up to 3 days. When ready to reheat, heat them in the air fryer at 350°F until warmed through.

Hands-On Time: 15 minutes
Cook Time: 10 minutes
Total Recipe Cost: $1.48

Serves 4

3 medium russet potatoes, peeled and shredded
½ teaspoon salt
¼ teaspoon ground black pepper
¼ teaspoon paprika

1 Preheat air fryer to 400°F.

2 Rinse shredded potatoes under cold water 3 minutes until water runs clear. This removes excess starches from the potatoes.

3 Drain well and squeeze out any excess moisture by wrapping potatoes in several layers of paper towels or a cheesecloth. Wring to remove extra water. Repeat if necessary.

4 Spray inside of air fryer with olive oil spray.

5 Spread potatoes inside air fryer in an even layer and season with salt, pepper, and paprika. Spray top of potatoes with olive oil spray.

6 Air fry 10 minutes, flipping halfway through the cooking time. Serve immediately.

PER SERVING

CALORIES: 109 | FAT: 0g | PROTEIN: 2g | SODIUM: 296mg | FIBER: 2g | CARBOHYDRATES: 25g | SUGAR: 2g

Two-Ingredient Pumpkin Muffins

This recipe is for those times when you need something easy and quick. I love this simple shortcut—using a box of cake mix and a can of pumpkin—for making homemade pumpkin muffins in the air fryer. If you can't find spice cake mix, vanilla cake mix may be used instead.

Hands-On Time: 15 minutes
Cook Time: 15 minutes
Total Recipe Cost: $3.42

Serves 6

1 (16.5-ounce) box spice cake mix
1 (15-ounce) can pure pumpkin

1 Preheat air fryer to 370°F. Grease a six-hole silicone egg mold and set aside.

2 In a medium bowl, combine cake mix and pumpkin.

3 Scoop batter into prepared egg mold and place egg mold inside air fryer.

4 Air fry 15 minutes. Let muffins cool on a cooling rack for 10 minutes before serving.

PER SERVING

CALORIES: 343 | **FAT:** 6g | **PROTEIN:** 3g | **SODIUM:** 483mg | **FIBER:** 3g | **CARBOHYDRATES:** 68g | **SUGAR:** 36g

3

Appetizers and Snacks

The air fryer really shines when it comes to making appetizers. Many favorite restaurant appetizers are deep-fried—which is why they taste so good! Luckily, the air fryer is amazing at making traditionally deep-fried foods extra crispy and full of flavor without all of that extra oil. In this chapter, you will find tasty appetizers like Onion Rings and Potato Skins. You will also learn how to make homemade Tortilla Chips, Fried Pickles, Crab Rangoon, and Pull-Apart Pizza Bread!

Onion Rings

Make sure to take the time to freeze the onions before cooking. It helps keep the batter on the onions as they cook. Leftover Onion Rings can be reheated in the air fryer at 300°F until warmed.

Hands-On Time: 20 minutes
Cook Time: 10 minutes (per batch)
Total Recipe Cost: $2.37

Serves 4

- 2 large sweet yellow onions, peeled and sliced into ½"-thick rings
- ¾ cup all-purpose flour
- 1 teaspoon garlic powder
- 1 teaspoon onion powder
- ½ teaspoon salt
- 2 large eggs
- 2 tablespoons whole milk
- 2 cups panko bread crumbs

1 Arrange onion slices on a baking sheet in a single layer and freeze 30 minutes.

2 Preheat air fryer to 370°F.

3 In a medium shallow bowl, combine flour, garlic powder, onion powder, and salt.

4 In a second medium shallow bowl, whisk together eggs and milk until well combined.

5 Fill a third medium shallow bowl with bread crumbs.

6 Dredge onion slices in flour mixture to evenly coat. Next, dip in egg mixture and shake off any excess. Finally, dip in bread crumbs, flipping to evenly coat.

7 Working in batches, arrange coated onion slices in a single layer inside air fryer and spray onion slices with olive oil spray.

8 Air fry 10 minutes, flipping halfway through the cooking time, until golden brown. Serve.

PER SERVING

CALORIES: 255 | **FAT:** 3g | **PROTEIN:** 9g | **SODIUM:** 308mg | **FIBER:** 2g | **CARBOHYDRATES:** 47g | **SUGAR:** 5g

Jalapeño Poppers

Enjoy this popular appetizer at home with this delicious recipe. When selecting jalapeños, choose larger ones because they tend to hold the filling best.

Hands-On Time: 15 minutes
Cook Time: 8 minutes
Total Recipe Cost: $2.25

Serves 4

4 ounces cream cheese, softened
¼ cup shredded sharp Cheddar cheese
1 teaspoon garlic powder
½ teaspoon onion powder
6 large jalapeños, sliced lengthwise with stems and seeds removed
¼ cup panko bread crumbs
1 tablespoon salted butter, melted

WANT THEM EXTRA SPICY?

If you like extra-spicy Jalapeño Poppers, reserve some of the seeds from the center of the jalapeños and mix them into the cream cheese mixture. It will add an extra kick!

1 Preheat air fryer to 370°F.

2 In a small bowl, combine cream cheese, Cheddar cheese, garlic powder, and onion powder. Mix well until fully combined.

3 Use a spoon to fill each jalapeño half with cheese mixture.

4 In a separate small bowl, combine bread crumbs and melted butter. Mix together with a fork until fully combined.

5 Gently press bread crumb mixture on top of each filled jalapeño half.

6 Carefully place jalapeño halves inside air fryer and spray jalapeño halves with oil.

7 Air fry 8 minutes until bread crumbs are golden brown. Serve.

PER SERVING (SERVING SIZE: 3 POPPERS)

CALORIES: 185 | FAT: 13g | PROTEIN: 5g | SODIUM: 163mg | FIBER: 1g | CARBOHYDRATES: 8g | SUGAR: 2g

Ham and Cheese Bites

Ham and cheese wrapped in puff pastry is out-of-this-world good. This dish comes out looking fancy, but it takes very little time to prep and cook.

Hands-On Time: 15 minutes
Cook Time: 8 minutes
Total Recipe Cost: $4.63

Serves 5

1 sheet frozen puff pastry, thawed
6 (1-ounce) slices honey ham
6 (1-ounce) slices Swiss cheese

MAKE THEM AHEAD OF TIME
Ham and Cheese Bites may be prepared and refrigerated up to 24 hours before air frying. Take them out and let them come to room temperature prior to cooking.

1 Preheat air fryer to 400°F.

2 Roll out puff pastry and top with an even layer of ham. Top ham with an even layer of cheese.

3 Roll pastry into a log, pinching the seams with your fingers to seal. Cut log into ten 1" slices.

4 Spray inside of air fryer with olive oil spray. Place pastry slices inside air fryer, spaced ½" apart. Spray top of each with olive oil spray.

5 Air fry 8 minutes, flipping halfway through the cooking time. Serve.

PER SERVING (SERVING SIZE: 2 BITES)

CALORIES: 444 | **FAT:** 28g | **PROTEIN:** 19g | **SODIUM:** 453mg | **FIBER:** 1g | **CARBOHYDRATES:** 27g | **SUGAR:** 1g

Stuffed Mushrooms

This recipe features tender baby bella mushrooms stuffed with pork sausage, cheese, and garlic! This affordable appetizer will make you feel extra fancy without overspending.

Hands-On Time: 15 minutes
Cook Time: 8 minutes (per batch)
Total Recipe Cost: $4.16

Serves 4

- ½ pound baby bella mushrooms
- ½ pound pork sausage, cooked
- ¼ cup grated Parmesan cheese, divided
- 4 ounces cream cheese, softened
- 1 teaspoon minced garlic
- ½ teaspoon salt

1 Preheat air fryer to 390°F. Remove mushroom stems.

2 In the bowl of a food processor, combine mushroom stems, sausage, ⅛ cup Parmesan, cream cheese, garlic, and salt. Process until finely chopped, about 20 seconds.

3 Use a spoon to fill each mushroom cap with prepared filling.

4 Sprinkle top of each mushroom cap with remaining ⅛ cup Parmesan.

5 Working in batches, carefully place mushrooms inside air fryer in a single layer. Spray mushroom tops with olive oil spray.

6 Air fry 8 minutes until tender and golden brown. Serve.

PER SERVING

CALORIES: 382 | **FAT:** 31g | **PROTEIN:** 13g | **SODIUM:** 1,070mg | **FIBER:** 0g | **CARBOHYDRATES:** 5g | **SUGAR:** 2g

Sweet Potato Chips

Healthier than the traditional potato chip, these Sweet Potato Chips are air fried with very little oil. A bit of brown sugar is added to bring out the sweetness of the sweet potato, but it may be omitted if desired.

Hands-On Time: 35 minutes
Cook Time: 28 minutes
Total Recipe Cost: $1.00

Serves 4

- 1 large sweet potato, peeled and sliced into ⅛"-thick chips
- 2 tablespoons olive oil
- 1 teaspoon salt
- 1 teaspoon packed light brown sugar
- ½ teaspoon ground black pepper
- ¼ teaspoon paprika
- ⅛ teaspoon cayenne pepper

HOW TO STORE SWEET POTATO CHIPS

Sweet Potato Chips should be fully cooled prior to storing in an airtight container at room temperature for up to 3 days.

1 In a medium bowl with cold water, soak potato slices 20 minutes. Rinse and pat dry.

2 Preheat air fryer to 360°F.

3 In a medium bowl, combine potato slices, oil, salt, brown sugar, black pepper, paprika, and cayenne pepper. Mix well.

4 Place coated potato slices inside air fryer all at once.

5 Air fry 28 minutes, shaking or turning every 5 minutes, until chips are crispy and no longer soft. Serve.

PER SERVING

CALORIES: 95 | FAT: 7g | PROTEIN: 1g | SODIUM: 592mg | FIBER: 1g | CARBOHYDRATES: 9g | SUGAR: 3g

Tortilla Chips

These Tortilla Chips are incredibly easy to make in an air fryer, and taste just like the ones from your favorite restaurant serving Mexican food. This recipe calls for small corn tortillas, but large corn tortillas may be used and cut into smaller pieces.

Hands-On Time: 15 minutes
Cook Time: 7 minutes (per batch)
Total Recipe Cost: $2.70

Serves 4

16 (6") corn tortillas
1 teaspoon salt

1 Preheat air fryer to 350°F.

2 Cut each tortilla into six triangles.

3 Spray inside of air fryer with olive oil spray.

4 Place tortilla pieces inside air fryer in a single layer. Spray with additional oil and sprinkle with salt (you may need to work in batches).

5 Air fry 7 minutes, shaking or turning twice during the cooking time, until chips are crispy. Serve.

PER SERVING

CALORIES: 247 | **FAT:** 3g | **PROTEIN:** 6g | **SODIUM:** 632mg | **FIBER:** 7g | **CARBOHYDRATES:** 51g | **SUGAR:** 1g

Potato Chips

This simple and delicious recipe will have homemade Potato Chips ready in under an hour. If the chips fly around in the air fryer, place a metal cooling rack or small oven-safe plate on top to hold them down.

Hands-On Time: 15 minutes
Cook Time: 25 minutes
Total Recipe Cost: $0.79

Serves 4

1 large russet potato, sliced into ⅛"-thick slices
4 tablespoons olive oil
½ teaspoon salt

1 Preheat air fryer to 360°F.

2 In a medium bowl, combine potato slices, oil, and salt. Toss to coat evenly.

3 Place potato slices inside air fryer and air fry 25 minutes, shaking or turning twice during the cooking time. Serve.

PER SERVING

CALORIES: 191 | **FAT:** 13g | **PROTEIN:** 2g | **SODIUM:** 301mg | **FIBER:** 2g | **CARBOHYDRATES:** 16g | **SUGAR:** 1g

Pigs in a Blanket

This fun appetizer is easy to make in an air fryer, and gets extra crispy around the edges. They'll be a hit at your next party!

Hands-On Time: 15 minutes
Cook Time: 5 minutes (per batch)
Total Recipe Cost: $3.41

Serves 6

1 (8-ounce) can refrigerated crescent roll dough
24 cocktail-sized smoked sausage links (14 ounces total)

1 Unroll crescent roll dough and cut each triangle into thirds lengthwise.

2 Preheat air fryer to 320°F.

3 Place sausages on the wider end of each piece of dough. Roll dough around sausages and pinch to adhere dough.

4 Spray inside of air fryer and each prepared Pig in a Blanket with olive oil spray.

5 Working in batches, arrange Pigs in a Blanket in a single layer inside air fryer.

6 Air fry 5 minutes until dough is golden brown. Serve.

PER SERVING (SERVING SIZE: 4 PIECES)

CALORIES: 332 | FAT: 24g | PROTEIN: 11g | SODIUM: 944mg |
FIBER: 0g | CARBOHYDRATES: 17g | SUGAR: 4g

Crab Rangoon

This Crab Rangoon recipe features crabmeat, cream cheese, and green onions wrapped in wonton wrappers and air fried to perfection. Making Crab Rangoon at home is quite easy. Once you get the hang of working with the wonton wrappers, you will be able to enjoy this appetizer any time the craving strikes!

Hands-On Time: 25 minutes
Cook Time: 10 minutes (per batch)
Total Recipe Cost: $9.58

Serves 4

1 (6-ounce) can crabmeat, drained
4 ounces cream cheese, softened
1 medium green onion, thinly sliced
1 teaspoon Worcestershire sauce
¼ teaspoon garlic powder
16 wonton wrappers
½ cup Thai sweet chili sauce

1   Preheat air fryer to 350°F.

2   In a medium bowl, combine crabmeat, cream cheese, green onion, Worcestershire sauce, and garlic powder. Mix well.

3   Fill each wonton wrapper with 1 tablespoon filling.

4   Dip your finger in warm water and brush it around edges of a wonton wrapper to moisten. Bring all four corners of the wrapper to the center, pressing the adjacent edges together to seal and make a small purse shape. Repeat with remaining wonton wrappers.

5   Spray inside of air fryer with olive oil spray. Arrange wontons in a single layer inside air fryer, spaced ½" apart, and spray tops with olive oil spray (you may need to work in batches).

6   Air fry 10 minutes until golden brown. Serve warm with chili sauce for dipping.

PER SERVING (SERVING SIZE: 4 WONTONS)

CALORIES: 297 | FAT: 9g | PROTEIN: 10g | SODIUM: 959mg | FIBER: 1g | CARBOHYDRATES: 39g | SUGAR: 19g

Bacon-Wrapped Smoked Sausages

The combination of savory bacon and smoked sausage mixed with brown sugar and melted butter makes for an appetizer that will please even the pickiest of eaters!

Hands-On Time: 15 minutes
Cook Time: 14 minutes
Total Recipe Cost: $6.92

Serves 6

10 slices bacon
30 mini smoked sausages (about 16 ounces total)
½ cup unsalted butter, melted
½ cup packed light brown sugar

1 Preheat air fryer to 340°F.

2 Cut each slice of bacon into thirds. Wrap each piece of sausage with bacon and secure with a toothpick.

3 Place wrapped sausages in a 7" cake pan.

4 In a small bowl, whisk together melted butter and brown sugar.

5 Pour butter mixture over sausages. Place cake pan inside air fryer.

6 Air fry 14 minutes until bacon is cooked. Serve.

PER SERVING (SERVING SIZE: 5 SAUSAGES)

CALORIES: 478 | FAT: 39g | PROTEIN: 15g | SODIUM: 1,031mg | FIBER: 0g | CARBOHYDRATES: 13g | SUGAR: 12g

Zucchini Bread

Use up one of summer's most abundant vegetables in this savory quick bread recipe. Zucchini Bread is extremely versatile and tastes great on its own or with chocolate chips mixed into the batter.

Hands-On Time: 20 minutes
Cook Time: 25 minutes
Total Recipe Cost: $1.55

Serves 4

1½ cups all-purpose flour
¾ cup granulated sugar
½ cup vegetable oil
2 large eggs
¼ teaspoon ground cinnamon
½ teaspoon baking powder
½ teaspoon baking soda
½ teaspoon salt
½ teaspoon vanilla extract
1 cup shredded zucchini

1 Preheat air fryer to 320°F. Grease two mini loaf pans and set aside.

2 In a large bowl, combine flour, sugar, oil, eggs, cinnamon, baking powder, baking soda, salt, and vanilla. Mix well.

3 Fold in zucchini. Evenly divide batter between prepared pans.

4 Air fry 25 minutes until a toothpick inserted in the center of bread comes out clean.

5 Let bread cool on a cooling rack for 15 minutes prior to serving.

PER SERVING

CALORIES: 606 | FAT: 29g | PROTEIN: 9g | SODIUM: 547mg | FIBER: 2g | CARBOHYDRATES: 75g | SUGAR: 38g

MAKE MUFFINS!

This Zucchini Bread may also be prepared as muffins. Simply pour batter into a six-hole silicone egg mold and air fry 14 minutes at 320°F.

Honey-Goat Cheese Balls

Honey-Goat Cheese Balls are the perfect addition to a cheese plate. Serve them with buttery crackers. Make sure to take them out of the air fryer just as they start to turn brown. If cooked too long, the cheese balls will begin to lose their shape.

Hands-On Time: 15 minutes
Cook Time: 4 minutes (per batch)
Total Recipe Cost: $6.86

Serves 5

1 (8-ounce) chèvre (goat cheese) log, softened
¼ cup honey
½ cup all-purpose flour
1 large egg, beaten
¾ cup panko bread crumbs

1 Line a cookie sheet with parchment paper and set aside.

2 In a small bowl, mix together chèvre and honey until well combined.

3 Scoop ten golf ball–sized balls of chèvre mixture and place on prepared cookie sheet. Place cookie sheet in freezer 45 minutes.

4 Preheat air fryer to 390°F.

5 In three separate medium bowls, place flour, egg, and bread crumbs. Dredge balls in flour. Then dip in egg, shaking off any excess, followed by bread crumbs.

6 Spray inside of air fryer with olive oil spray.

7 Working in batches, place coated balls inside air fryer, spaced ½" apart. Spray each ball with olive oil spray.

8 Air fry 4 minutes just until golden brown. Serve.

PER SERVING (SERVING SIZE: 2 BALLS)

CALORIES: 255 | FAT: 10g | PROTEIN: 12g | SODIUM: 241mg | FIBER: 0g | CARBOHYDRATES: 29g | SUGAR: 14g

Peach Bread

Like Banana Bread (see recipe in Chapter 2) and Zucchini Bread (see recipe in this chapter), Peach Bread is a simple quick bread with fresh peaches baked inside. Nectarines or apricots may be used in place of peaches in this recipe.

Hands-On Time: 15 minutes
Cook Time: 25 minutes
Total Recipe Cost: $2.46

Serves 4

2 large peaches, peeled and pitted
¾ cup all-purpose flour
¼ cup sour cream
1 large egg
3 tablespoons packed light brown sugar
3 tablespoons granulated sugar
2 tablespoons unsalted butter, melted
½ teaspoon baking powder
½ teaspoon baking soda
½ teaspoon vanilla extract
¼ teaspoon salt

1 Preheat air fryer to 320°F. Grease two mini loaf pans and set aside.

2 Place peaches in the bowl of a food processor and purée 20 seconds.

3 In a medium bowl, combine flour, sour cream, egg, brown sugar, granulated sugar, melted butter, baking powder, baking soda, vanilla, and salt. Mix well.

4 Fold in peaches.

5 Evenly divide batter between two prepared pans.

6 Air fry 25 minutes until a toothpick inserted in the center of bread comes out clean.

7 Let bread cool on a cooling rack for 15 minutes prior to serving.

PER SERVING

CALORIES: 278 | FAT: 9g | PROTEIN: 5g | SODIUM: 390mg | FIBER: 2g | CARBOHYDRATES: 43g | SUGAR: 24g

Jalapeño Cheese Crisps

Crisped Parmesan cheese with spicy jalapeños make an easy appetizer or snack. Use a spatula to lift them up and out of the air fryer after they cook. If your air fryer does not have a nonstick coating, then you will want to spray olive oil inside the air fryer prior to cooking the cheese crisps.

Hands-On Time: 10 minutes
Cook Time: 15 minutes
Total Recipe Cost: $3.20

Serves 4

2 large jalapeños, stems and seeds removed, sliced into ½"-thick circles
1 cup grated Parmesan cheese
½ teaspoon salt
½ teaspoon paprika
⅛ teaspoon ground black pepper

IS YOUR CHEESE SPREADING?

When air frying cheese crisps, they have a tendency to spread and get gooey before crisping up. Use a spatula to scrape all of the cheese together when flipping. Cheese crisps are done when they turn crispy and are no longer gooey.

1 Preheat air fryer to 340°F.

2 Arrange sliced jalapeños in a single layer inside air fryer. Air fry 7 minutes. Remove from air fryer and set aside.

3 In a small bowl, mix together cheese, salt, paprika, and pepper.

4 Spray inside of air fryer with olive oil spray. Scoop heaping tablespoons of cheese mixture and place inside air fryer, spaced ½" apart.

5 Press a jalapeño slice in the center of each cheese mound. Air fry 8 minutes, flipping halfway through the cooking time. Serve warm.

PER SERVING

CALORIES: 107 | **FAT:** 6g | **PROTEIN:** 7g | **SODIUM:** 741mg | **FIBER:** 0g | **CARBOHYDRATES:** 4g | **SUGAR:** 0g

Soft Pretzels

Homemade Soft Pretzels take some time to prepare, but they are so worth it! I like to make a big batch and freeze the extras for when a craving hits.

Hands-On Time: 1 hour, 30 minutes
Cook Time: 8 minutes (per batch)
Total Recipe Cost: $1.41

Serves 10

1¼ cups warm (110°F–115°F) water

2 tablespoons active dry yeast

5 cups all-purpose flour

½ cup granulated sugar

1 tablespoon vegetable oil

1½ teaspoons salt

4 cups hot water

½ cup baking soda

½ teaspoon coarse sea salt

TIPS FOR WORKING WITH PRETZEL DOUGH

If the dough is sticking to your fingers while kneading, slowly mix in more flour until it's no longer sticky. If the dough is too dry and falling apart, mix in 1–2 tablespoons additional water.

1 In a large bowl, whisk together warm water and yeast until yeast is dissolved. Let mixture sit 10 minutes until frothy.

2 Mix in flour, sugar, oil, and salt. Continue to mix until rough dough forms.

3 Transfer dough onto a clean, floured surface and knead 8 minutes until dough is smooth and no longer sticky. If dough is too sticky, add more flour until dough no longer sticks to your fingers.

4 Place dough in an oil-greased large bowl and turn dough to fully coat with oil. Cover bowl with a clean dish towel. Let dough sit in a warm spot and allow to rise until dough has doubled in size, about 1 hour. (The dough will take longer to rise if your kitchen is cold.)

5 Preheat air fryer to 320°F.

6 Once dough has doubled in size, place it on a clean, lightly floured surface and divide into ten equal pieces.

7 Roll each piece into a 12"-long snake shape and twist into a pretzel shape.

8 Place formed pretzels on a baking sheet and spray with olive oil spray. Cover with a clean dish towel and let rise 45 minutes.

9 In a small bowl, whisk together hot water and baking soda until baking soda is dissolved. Dip each formed pretzel into baking soda mixture and set aside.

10 Spray inside of air fryer with olive oil spray. Working in batches, arrange pretzels in an even layer inside air fryer, spaced ½" apart.

11 Spray pretzels with olive oil spray and sprinkle with sea salt.

12 Air fry 8 minutes until golden brown and cooked throughout. Let cool on a cooling rack 10 minutes. Serve.

PER SERVING

CALORIES: 286 | FAT: 2g | PROTEIN: 7g | SODIUM: 731mg | FIBER: 2g | CARBOHYDRATES: 59g | SUGAR: 10g

Kale Chips

Kale Chips are a great way to feed that crunchy and salty craving in a healthier way. You can easily make them yourself in your air fryer with fresh kale, a bit of oil, and lots of spices.

Hands-On Time: 12 minutes
Cook Time: 5 minutes (per batch)
Total Recipe Cost: $2.06

Serves 4

4 cups kale, stems removed and leaves torn into 3" pieces
2 tablespoons olive oil
1 teaspoon salt
½ teaspoon garlic powder
¼ teaspoon ground black pepper
¼ teaspoon onion powder

CAN YOU MAKE THESE AHEAD?
Kale Chips are best eaten on the same day they are cooked. However, they can be stored at room temperature in an airtight container for 2 days.

1 Preheat air fryer to 360°F.

2 Place kale in a large bowl and drizzle with oil. Using clean hands, massage oil into kale leaves until evenly coated.

3 Sprinkle salt, garlic powder, pepper, and onion powder over kale and stir.

4 Working in batches, arrange kale in an even layer inside air fryer. Air fry 5 minutes, shaking or turning once during the cooking time.

5 Spread chips on a cookie sheet in an even layer to cool. Serve.

PER SERVING

CALORIES: 69 | FAT: 7g | PROTEIN: 1g | SODIUM: 587mg | FIBER: 1g | CARBOHYDRATES: 2g | SUGAR: 0g

Potato Skins

Make these crispy, crowd-pleasing Potato Skins with just four ingredients! You are not going to believe how simple it is to make your own Potato Skins at home.

Hands-On Time: 10 minutes
Cook Time: 25 minutes
Total Recipe Cost: $9.80

Serves 6

6 small baking potatoes
½ cup shredded sharp Cheddar cheese
½ cup crumbled cooked bacon
¼ cup thinly sliced chives

1 Preheat air fryer to 400°F.

2 Poke potatoes all over with a fork. Place potatoes in a single layer inside air fryer. Air fry 20 minutes.

3 Remove potatoes from air fryer and slice in half. Scoop flesh out from inside of potatoes, leaving some around the edges of each potato skin.

4 Place potato skins back inside air fryer, skin-side down, and sprinkle with cheese and bacon. Air fry an additional 5 minutes.

5 Sprinkle each potato skin with chives prior to serving.

PER SERVING (SERVING SIZE: 2 POTATO SKINS)

CALORIES: 181 | FAT: 7g | PROTEIN: 9g | SODIUM: 286mg | FIBER: 2g | CARBOHYDRATES: 20g | SUGAR: 1g

Apple Chips

These Apple Chips are the perfect healthy snack, and they are even better when paired with the three-ingredient peanut butter dip in this recipe! If the chips start to stick together, pull them apart before continuing to air fry.

Hands-On Time: 15 minutes
Cook Time: 16 minutes
Total Recipe Cost: $1.10

Serves 4

- 1 large Granny Smith apple, cored
- ½ teaspoon ground cinnamon
- ¼ cup plain Greek yogurt
- 1 tablespoon creamy natural peanut butter
- 1 teaspoon honey

STORING LEFTOVERS
Uneaten Apple Chips can be stored at room temperature in an airtight container for 2 days. Uneaten dip can be stored in the refrigerator for 3 days.

1 Preheat air fryer to 300°F.

2 Slice apple into ¼"-thick slices and sprinkle with cinnamon.

3 Arrange apples in an even layer inside air fryer. A little bit of overlapping is okay.

4 Air fry 16 minutes, shaking or turning every 2–3 minutes during the cooking time, until apple slices begin to brown around the edges.

5 Remove apple slices from air fryer and set them on a plate to continue to crisp.

6 In a small bowl, whisk together yogurt, peanut butter, and honey. Serve apples with yogurt dip.

PER SERVING

CALORIES: 73 | FAT: 3g | PROTEIN: 2g | SODIUM: 6mg | FIBER: 2g | CARBOHYDRATES: 10g | SUGAR: 7g

Pull-Apart Pizza Bread

Pull-Apart Pizza Bread is made by coating balls of dough in a savory mixture of seasonings and then pouring melted butter on top before air frying. Melt mozzarella cheese at the end for a yummy flavor combination. Toppings like sliced black olives or small pepperoni may also be added into the Parmesan cheese mixture.

Hands-On Time: 15 minutes
Cook Time: 14 minutes
Total Recipe Cost: $5.53

Serves 6

1 (13.8-ounce) can
    refrigerated pizza dough
½ cup grated Parmesan
    cheese
1 tablespoon Italian
    seasoning
½ teaspoon chili powder
½ teaspoon garlic powder
¼ cup unsalted butter,
    melted
½ cup shredded mozzarella
    cheese

1 Preheat air fryer to 390°F. Grease a Bundt pan and set aside.

2 Remove dough from can and cut into six 1" chunks.

3 In a large bowl, combine dough chunks, Parmesan, Italian seasoning, chili powder, and garlic powder. Mix well.

4 Arrange coated dough chunks in prepared pan. Pour melted butter on top and place pan inside air fryer.

5 Air fry 14 minutes. Sprinkle mozzarella over bread and air fry 1 more minute until cheese is melted.

6 Place pan on a cooling rack and let bread cool 10 minutes before serving.

PER SERVING

CALORIES: 292 | **FAT:** 13g | **PROTEIN:** 10g | **SODIUM:** 602mg | **FIBER:** 1g | **CARBOHYDRATES:** 33g | **SUGAR:** 4g

Pizza Pockets

Pizza Pockets make a great lunch or dinner and are perfect when paired with a simple green salad.

Hands-On Time: 10 minutes
Cook Time: 12 minutes
Total Recipe Cost: $4.85

Serves 4

1 sheet frozen puff pastry, thawed
¼ cup pizza sauce
½ cup shredded mozzarella cheese
½ cup pepperoni slices

1 Preheat air fryer to 350°F.

2 Roll out puff pastry and slice into four equal strips.

3 Coat half of each pastry strip with pizza sauce. Sprinkle with cheese and top with pepperoni.

4 Fold each pastry strip in half and seal edges using the tines of a fork. Place inside air fryer.

5 Air fry 12 minutes until golden brown. Serve.

PER SERVING

CALORIES: 479 | FAT: 33g | PROTEIN: 11g | SODIUM: 607mg | FIBER: 1g | CARBOHYDRATES: 30g | SUGAR: 1g

Fried Pickles

These Fried Pickles come out so good and need only two ingredients. If you can't find extra-crispy seasoning mix, then any traditional crispy coating intended for chicken will work.

Hands-On Time: 12 minutes
Cook Time: 9 minutes (per batch)
Total Recipe Cost: $2.98

Serves 6

1 (5-ounce) package extra-crispy seasoning and coating mix, like Shake 'n Bake
1 (16-ounce) jar dill pickle chips, drained

1 Preheat air fryer to 400°F.

2 Place seasoning mix and pickles in a gallon-sized zip-top plastic bag. Shake bag to evenly coat pickles with seasoning mix.

3 Spray inside of air fryer with olive oil spray. Arrange pickles in a single layer inside air fryer (you may need to work in batches).

4 Air fry 9 minutes. Serve.

PER SERVING

CALORIES: 76 | FAT: 0g | PROTEIN: 1g | SODIUM: 794mg | FIBER: 0g | CARBOHYDRATES: 16g | SUGAR: 1g

Mozzarella Sticks

Make your own crispy, gooey, and cheesy Mozzarella Sticks at home using your air fryer!
You'll love how easy it is to make these restaurant-quality appetizers!

Hands-On Time: 20 minutes
Cook Time: 8 minutes
Total Recipe Cost: $6.90

Serves 6

12 (1-ounce) mozzarella cheese sticks
¼ cup all-purpose flour
2 large eggs, beaten
1¾ cups panko bread crumbs
1½ tablespoons Italian seasoning
¾ teaspoon salt
½ teaspoon ground black pepper

1 Place cheese sticks on a cookie sheet, spaced apart so they are not touching. Freeze a minimum of 3 hours.

2 In three separate medium shallow bowls, place flour, eggs, and bread crumbs.

3 Add Italian seasoning, salt, and pepper to bowl of bread crumbs. Mix.

4 Line a separate cookie sheet with foil and spray with olive oil spray.

5 Dredge each frozen cheese stick in flour until evenly coated. Then dip in eggs until completely coated, shaking off any excess. Finally, dip in bread crumbs, making sure entire cheese stick is evenly coated.

6 Lay coated cheese sticks on prepared cookie sheet in an even layer with space between each so they don't touch. Freeze 10 minutes. Do not discard breading ingredients.

7 Preheat air fryer to 390°F.

8 Remove chilled cheese sticks from freezer and dip in remaining eggs and then in bread crumbs.

9 Spray inside of air fryer with olive oil spray. Arrange cheese sticks in an even layer inside air fryer, spaced ½" apart.

10 Air fry 8 minutes, flipping halfway through the cooking time. Serve.

PER SERVING (SERVING SIZE: 2 MOZZARELLA STICKS)

CALORIES: 292 | FAT: 14g | PROTEIN: 19g | SODIUM: 785mg | FIBER: 0g | CARBOHYDRATES: 21g | SUGAR: 1g

4

Side Dishes

Side dishes can really make a meal shine. This chapter will share many frugal side dishes that taste amazing when cooked in an air fryer. Included in this chapter are healthy and delicious vegetable side dishes along with several ways to prepare a potato in the air fryer that will fill you up and have you coming back for seconds. Some of the tasty side dishes you will make are homemade Cheddar Drop Biscuits, Potato Wedges, Carrot Fries, Maple Bacon Brussels Sprouts, and Garlic Toast.

French Fries

Make your own delicious crispy French Fries at home with this easy recipe. Make sure to not skip the step of soaking the potatoes. It makes all the difference in the texture of the fries.

Hands-On Time: 10 minutes
Cook Time: 16 minutes (per batch)
Total Recipe Cost: $2.08

Serves 4

4 medium russet potatoes, cut into ¼"-thick strips
2 tablespoons olive oil
1 teaspoon salt

KEEPING FRIES WARM

When making French Fries in an air fryer, you will need to work in batches. I recommend storing cooked French Fries in a warm oven until all batches have been cooked.

1 Fill a medium bowl with cold water and soak cut potatoes 1 hour, changing the water every 20 minutes.

2 Rinse and drain potatoes. Pat dry.

3 Preheat air fryer to 380°F.

4 In a large bowl, toss potatoes in oil and salt.

5 Working in batches, spread potatoes in an even layer inside air fryer. Air fry 16 minutes until crispy, shaking or turning halfway through the cooking time. Serve.

PER SERVING

CALORIES: 227 | FAT: 7g | PROTEIN: 5g | SODIUM: 605mg | FIBER: 4g | CARBOHYDRATES: 37g | SUGAR: 2g

Air-Fried Artichokes

These Air-Fried Artichokes are so good! They come out with a much different texture than the steamed version. With this cooking method, the artichokes are slightly crispy around the edges, and the artichoke hearts have a nice smoky flavor.

Hands-On Time: 10 minutes
Cook Time: 15 minutes
Total Recipe Cost: $5.25

Serves 4

2 medium artichokes
2 tablespoons olive oil
1 tablespoon lemon juice
1 teaspoon garlic salt
¼ teaspoon ground black pepper

AIR FRYING DIFFERENT SIZES OF ARTICHOKES

You can air fry larger artichokes as long as they will fit inside your air fryer. Simply increase the air fry time to 20 minutes.

1 Preheat air fryer to 340°F.

2 Trim ¼" off the top of each artichoke and trim stem so they will fit inside air fryer. Cut each artichoke in half.

3 In a small bowl, whisk together oil, lemon juice, garlic salt, and pepper.

4 Brush oil mixture over cut side of artichokes so it drips down in between leaves.

5 Air fry 15 minutes until artichokes are fork-tender. Serve.

PER SERVING

CALORIES: 90 | FAT: 7g | PROTEIN: 2g | SODIUM: 550mg | FIBER: 4g | CARBOHYDRATES: 7g | SUGAR: 1g

Carrot Fries

Carrot Fries are a fun alternative to boiled or roasted carrots. They come out extra crispy with a tender center, and the seasonings in this recipe add a nice flavor.

Hands-On Time: 12 minutes
Cook Time: 16 minutes (per batch)
Total Recipe Cost: $1.10

Serves 4

1 pound carrots, peeled and sliced into wedges (2" long × ¼" wide)
2 tablespoons olive oil
½ teaspoon garlic salt
¼ teaspoon ground black pepper

1 Preheat air fryer to 350°F.

2 In a medium bowl, combine carrots, oil, garlic salt, and pepper. Toss to coat evenly.

3 Place carrots in a single layer inside air fryer (you may need to work in batches).

4 Air fry 16 minutes, shaking or turning halfway through the cooking time. Serve warm.

PER SERVING

CALORIES: 104 | FAT: 7g | PROTEIN: 1g | SODIUM: 320mg | FIBER: 3g | CARBOHYDRATES: 11g | SUGAR: 5g

Green Beans

I love these Green Beans as an easy and healthy side dish. They come out especially tasty when air fried alongside a minced shallot. Shallots are typically stored with the fresh garlic in the produce section of the grocery store.

Hands-On Time: 10 minutes
Cook Time: 8 minutes
Total Recipe Cost: $2.35

Serves 4

1 pound green beans, trimmed
1 large shallot, peeled and minced
2 tablespoons olive oil
½ teaspoon salt
¼ teaspoon ground black pepper

1 Preheat air fryer to 370°F.

2 In a medium bowl, combine all ingredients. Stir until evenly combined.

3 Place green beans inside air fryer.

4 Air fry 8 minutes, stirring halfway through the cooking time. Serve.

PER SERVING

CALORIES: 97 | FAT: 7g | PROTEIN: 2g | SODIUM: 297mg | FIBER: 3g | CARBOHYDRATES: 9g | SUGAR: 4g

Parmesan Zucchini Rounds

Zucchini rounds topped with Parmesan cheese come out of the air fryer perfectly tender with crispy cheese on top. They make an easy and healthy side dish that takes only 8 minutes to cook.

Hands-On Time: 12 minutes
Cook Time: 8 minutes (per batch)
Total Recipe Cost: $3.08

Serves 4

2 medium zucchini, sliced into ¼"-thick rounds
1 teaspoon garlic powder
½ teaspoon salt
¼ teaspoon ground black pepper
½ cup grated Parmesan cheese

1 Preheat air fryer to 370°F.

2 Spray inside of air fryer with olive oil spray. Arrange sliced zucchini inside air fryer in a single layer and sprinkle with garlic powder, salt, and pepper. Top with cheese (you may need to work in batches).

3 Air fry 8 minutes until cheese is golden brown. Serve.

PER SERVING

CALORIES: 71 | FAT: 3g | PROTEIN: 5g | SODIUM: 524mg | FIBER: 1g | CARBOHYDRATES: 5g | SUGAR: 2g

Zucchini Fries

This lighter take on the traditional French fry is covered with a delicious Parmesan cheese coating, adding an extra flavor that you won't get with regular French fries.

Hands-On Time: 17 minutes
Cook Time: 10 minutes (per batch)
Total Recipe Cost: $4.96

Serves 4

2 large eggs, beaten
1 cup grated Parmesan cheese
2 teaspoons garlic powder
1 teaspoon paprika
½ teaspoon ground black pepper
2 medium zucchini, cut into ½"-thick wedges

1 Preheat air fryer to 400°F.

2 Add beaten eggs into a small bowl.

3 In a second small bowl, mix together cheese, garlic powder, paprika, and pepper.

4 Dip zucchini in eggs, shaking off any excess. Next, dip in cheese mixture and coat evenly.

5 Spray inside of air fryer with olive oil spray. Arrange zucchini wedges in a single layer inside air fryer (you may need to work in batches).

6 Air fry 10 minutes until golden brown and fork-tender. Serve.

PER SERVING

CALORIES: 127 | FAT: 6g | PROTEIN: 9g | SODIUM: 373mg |
FIBER: 1g | CARBOHYDRATES: 7g | SUGAR: 3g

Potato Wedges

Potato Wedges are the thick and tasty cousin of French Fries (see recipe in this chapter). They require the same 1-hour soaking in cold water, but they are well worth the wait! Potato Wedges are best eaten right away, but if you want to save some for another day, reheat them in the air fryer at 400°F until warmed through.

Hands-On Time: 22 minutes
Cook Time: 15 minutes (per batch)
Total Recipe Cost: $3.39

Serves 4

4 medium russet potatoes, cut into ½"-thick wedges
2 tablespoons olive oil
2 tablespoons minced garlic
1 tablespoon minced fresh rosemary
1 teaspoon salt
¼ teaspoon ground black pepper

1 Fill a medium bowl with cold water and soak potato wedges 1 hour, changing water every 20 minutes. Rinse and dry potatoes well.

2 Preheat air fryer to 400°F.

3 In a medium bowl, combine potatoes, oil, garlic, rosemary, salt, and pepper. Mix well to evenly coat.

4 Arrange potatoes in an even layer inside of air fryer (you may need to work in batches).

5 Air fry 15 minutes until fork-tender. Serve.

PER SERVING

CALORIES: 234 | FAT: 7g | PROTEIN: 5g | SODIUM: 605mg | FIBER: 4g | CARBOHYDRATES: 39g | SUGAR: 2g

Seasoned Summer Squash

Yellow squash has a delicious flavor but is generally available only during the summer months. If you're preparing this dish during the off-season, you can substitute the yellow squash with zucchini.

Hands-On Time: 12 minutes
Cook Time: 8 minutes (per batch)
Total Recipe Cost: $1.99

Serves 4

2 medium yellow summer squash, cut into ¼"-thick rounds
2 tablespoons olive oil
1 teaspoon garlic powder
½ teaspoon salt
½ teaspoon dried parsley
¼ teaspoon ground black pepper

1. Preheat air fryer to 370°F.

2. In a medium bowl, combine squash, oil, garlic powder, salt, parsley, and pepper. Mix well.

3. Arrange squash in an even layer inside air fryer (you may need to work in batches).

4. Air fry 8 minutes until fork-tender. Serve.

PER SERVING

CALORIES: 77 | FAT: 7g | PROTEIN: 1g | SODIUM: 292mg | FIBER: 1g | CARBOHYDRATES: 4g | SUGAR: 2g

Corn on the Cob

Air-fried Corn on the Cob comes out similar to grilled corn. It has a great flavor with crispy edges

Hands-On Time: 5 minutes
Cook Time: 10 minutes
Total Recipe Cost: $1.70

Serves 4

4 medium ears corn, husks removed
½ teaspoon salt
¼ teaspoon ground black pepper

1. Preheat air fryer to 400°F.

2. Spray inside of air fryer with olive oil spray. Season corn with salt and pepper. Arrange corn in a single layer inside air fryer.

3. Air fry 10 minutes until kernels are tender. Serve.

PER SERVING

CALORIES: 87 | FAT: 1g | PROTEIN: 3g | SODIUM: 305mg | FIBER: 2g | CARBOHYDRATES: 19g | SUGAR: 6g

Root Vegetables

This dish is a delicious combination of onion, parsnip, baby carrots, and red potatoes. The fresh rosemary adds a bright flavor, and the air fryer makes everything nice and crisp on the outside. If you don't like the flavor of parsnip, an additional ½ pound baby carrots may be substituted.

Hands-On Time: 15 minutes
Cook Time: 15 minutes
Total Recipe Cost: $4.56

Serves 6

- 1 medium red onion, peeled and roughly chopped
- 1 medium parsnip, peeled and sliced
- ½ pound baby carrots
- 1 pound baby red potatoes, quartered
- 3 tablespoons olive oil
- 1 teaspoon minced fresh rosemary
- 1 teaspoon salt
- ½ teaspoon ground black pepper

1 Preheat air fryer to 400°F.

2 In a large bowl, combine all ingredients and mix well. Place mixture inside air fryer.

3 Air fry 15 minutes, shaking or turning halfway through the cooking time. Serve warm.

PER SERVING

CALORIES: 152 | FAT: 7g | PROTEIN: 2g | SODIUM: 429mg | FIBER: 4g | CARBOHYDRATES: 21g | SUGAR: 5g

Hasselback Potatoes

Hasselback Potatoes are baked potatoes with ridges cut in the top to allow for oil and seasonings to cook inside of the potatoes. In the air fryer, they come out perfectly tender and flavorful on the inside with a crispy skin.

Hands-On Time: 10 minutes
Cook Time: 15 minutes
Total Recipe Cost: $2.16

Serves 4

4 medium russet potatoes
2 tablespoons olive oil
1 teaspoon paprika
1 teaspoon salt
½ teaspoon ground black
  pepper

USING A DIFFERENT POTATO SIZE

Smaller potatoes can be used to make Hasselback Potatoes. Simply reduce the air fry time to 10 minutes or until the potatoes are fork-tender. Alternately, jumbo potatoes can be used by increasing the cook time to 20 minutes.

1 Preheat air fryer to 370°F.

2 Slice slits in top of each potato, coming ¾ of the way down through the potato. Place potatoes inside air fryer with slits facing up.

3 In a small bowl, whisk together oil, paprika, salt, and pepper. Brush oil mixture over each potato and in slits.

4 Air fry 15 minutes until potatoes are fork-tender. Serve.

PER SERVING

CALORIES: 229 | FAT: 7g | PROTEIN: 5g | SODIUM: 605mg | FIBER: 4g | CARBOHYDRATES: 38g | SUGAR: 2g

Pull-Apart Dinner Rolls

This recipe makes a wonderful small batch of dinner rolls that are large and fluffy. They taste great when paired with soup or pasta or served as sandwiches. Make sure to plan enough time to let the dough rise.

Hands-On Time: 20 minutes
Cook Time: 10 minutes
Total Recipe Cost: $0.50

Serves 4

½ cup plus 1 tablespoon warm (110°F–115°F) water
1 teaspoon active dry yeast
2 cups all-purpose flour
1 large egg yolk
2 tablespoons vegetable oil
⅛ cup granulated sugar
¾ teaspoon salt

ADDING MORE FLOUR

When working with bread dough, it is important to be flexible with the amount of flour used. If the dough is too sticky to work with, slowly add in extra flour by the tablespoonful until a better consistency is reached. This can be up to an additional ½ cup flour. If the dough becomes too dry, a small amount of water may be added to the dough.

1 In a large bowl, whisk together warm water and yeast until yeast is dissolved. Let sit 10 minutes until water becomes frothy.

2 Mix in flour, egg yolk, oil, sugar, and salt. Continue to mix until a dough is formed.

3 Pour dough onto a clean, floured surface and knead until dough is smooth and no longer sticky, about 8 minutes.

4 Place dough in an oil-greased large bowl and cover with a clean dish towel. Leave in a warm spot to rise 1 hour.

5 Grease a 7" cake pan.

6 Once dough has doubled in size, gently punch down dough and place on a clean, floured surface. Cut dough into four equal pieces and roll each into a round ball.

7 Place dough balls in prepared pan. Cover with a clean dish towel and let rise 45 minutes.

8 Preheat air fryer to 350°F.

9 Uncover pan and spray tops of dough with olive oil spray. Place pan inside air fryer.

10 Air fry 10 minutes. Let cool 10 minutes before serving.

PER SERVING

CALORIES: 330 | FAT: 8g | PROTEIN: 8g | SODIUM: 439mg | FIBER: 2g | CARBOHYDRATES: 55g | SUGAR: 6g

Parmesan Brussels Sprouts

Brussels sprouts in the air fryer come out perfectly crisp around the edges. This easy recipe yields excellent flavor with just a few seasonings and Parmesan cheese.

Hands-On Time: 10 minutes
Cook Time: 15 minutes
Total Recipe Cost: $3.19

Serves 4

1 pound Brussels sprouts, halved
½ cup grated Parmesan cheese
2 tablespoons olive oil
½ teaspoon garlic salt
¼ teaspoon ground black pepper

1 Preheat air fryer to 350°F.

2 In a medium bowl, combine Brussels sprouts, cheese, oil, garlic salt, and pepper. Toss to evenly coat.

3 Place Brussels sprouts inside air fryer and arrange in an even layer.

4 Air fry 15 minutes, shaking or turning halfway through the cooking time. Serve warm.

PER SERVING

CALORIES: 148 | **FAT:** 10g | **PROTEIN:** 6g | **SODIUM:** 491mg | **FIBER:** 3g | **CARBOHYDRATES:** 9g | **SUGAR:** 2g

Air-Fried Broccoli

This Air-Fried Broccoli comes out crispy and roasted to perfection. It's tossed in lemon juice and garlic seasoning before being air fried, giving it lots of flavor.

Hands-On Time: 10 minutes
Cook Time: 12 minutes
Total Recipe Cost: $1.38

Serves 4

1 pound broccoli florets
3 tablespoons olive oil
1 tablespoon lemon juice
1 teaspoon salt
1 teaspoon garlic powder

1 Preheat air fryer to 400°F.

2 In a large bowl, combine broccoli, oil, lemon juice, salt, and garlic powder. Toss to coat evenly.

3 Place broccoli inside air fryer.

4 Air fry 12 minutes, shaking or turning halfway through the cooking time. Serve.

PER SERVING

CALORIES: 116 | FAT: 10g | PROTEIN: 2g | SODIUM: 604mg | FIBER: 2g | CARBOHYDRATES: 5g | SUGAR: 1g

Maple Bacon Brussels Sprouts

This is a heavenly dish that will have you coming back for seconds! If you're using thin-cut bacon instead of thick-cut, mix in the bacon after cooking the sprouts for 5 minutes.

Hands-On Time: 10 minutes
Cook Time: 15 minutes
Total Recipe Cost: $4.28

Serves 4

1 pound Brussels sprouts, halved
2 slices thick-cut bacon, chopped
3 tablespoons olive oil
2 tablespoons pure maple syrup
1 teaspoon salt
¼ teaspoon ground black pepper

1 Preheat air fryer to 350°F.

2 In a medium bowl, combine Brussels sprouts and bacon.

3 In a small bowl, whisk together oil, maple syrup, salt, and pepper. Drizzle oil mixture over sprouts and stir until evenly coated.

4 Arrange Brussels sprouts inside air fryer.

5 Air fry 15 minutes, shaking or turning halfway through the cooking time. Serve.

PER SERVING

CALORIES: 210 | FAT: 15g | PROTEIN: 5g | SODIUM: 695mg | FIBER: 3g | CARBOHYDRATES: 14g | SUGAR: 8g

Baked Potatoes

These air-fried Baked Potatoes come out with crispy skin while being fork-tender on the inside! If you love traditional baked potatoes, you are going to love this version made in the air fryer!

Hands-On Time: 10 minutes
Cook Time: 40 minutes
Total Recipe Cost: $2.24

Serves 4

4 medium russet potatoes
⅛ cup olive oil
½ teaspoon salt
¼ teaspoon ground black
   pepper

KNOW WHEN YOUR POTATOES ARE DONE

This is one of those recipes that needs to be watched. Depending on the size of your potatoes and strength of your air fryer, the potatoes may need to be cooked for a little less or more time. It's best to test them toward the end by sticking a fork in them. If the fork slides into a potato easily, they are done.

1 Preheat air fryer to 400°F. Prick potatoes all over with the tines of a fork.

2 Rub oil over each potato and season with salt and pepper. Place potatoes inside air fryer.

3 Air fry 30 minutes, then carefully flip potatoes over and air fry an additional 10 minutes. Serve.

PER SERVING

CALORIES: 227 | FAT: 7g | PROTEIN: 5g | SODIUM: 314mg | FIBER: 4g | CARBOHYDRATES: 37g | SUGAR: 2g

Herbed Carrots

Make these flavor-packed carrots tonight! They come out crispy, fork-tender, and smothered with herbs! Don't use too much oil in this recipe, as it can cause the herbs to slide off the carrots and into the bottom of the air fryer. Mixing them well before putting them in the air fryer will help keep the herbs on the carrots.

Hands-On Time: 10 minutes
Cook Time: 10 minutes
Total Recipe Cost: $1.98

Serves 4

- 1 pound carrots, peeled and sliced into 2" rounds
- 3 tablespoons olive oil
- 1 teaspoon dried parsley
- 1 teaspoon dried oregano
- ¾ teaspoon salt
- ½ teaspoon ground thyme
- ¼ teaspoon ground black pepper

1 Preheat air fryer to 400°F.

2 Halve or quarter any thicker pieces of carrots so they are all approximately the same size.

3 In a medium bowl, combine carrots, oil, parsley, oregano, salt, thyme, and pepper. Mix until evenly coated.

4 Arrange carrots inside air fryer in an even layer. Some overlap is okay.

5 Air fry 10 minutes, shaking or turning halfway through the cooking time. Serve.

PER SERVING

CALORIES: 135 | **FAT:** 10g | **PROTEIN:** 1g | **SODIUM:** 512mg | **FIBER:** 3g | **CARBOHYDRATES:** 11g | **SUGAR:** 5g

Classic Biscuits

Whip up a batch of these Classic Biscuits to pair with soup or barbecue. They require just five ingredients and cook quickly in an air fryer. If you don't own a biscuit cutter, the top of a glass or jar, roughly 2" wide, may be used.

Hands-On Time: 20 minutes
Cook Time: 10 minutes (per batch)
Total Recipe Cost: $1.27

Serves 6

2½ cups all-purpose flour
4 teaspoons baking powder
½ teaspoon salt
¼ cup unsalted butter, cubed and chilled
1 cup cold whole milk

1   Preheat air fryer to 400°F.

2   In a large bowl, whisk together flour, baking powder, and salt.

3   Add in butter and mix together with a fork until flour forms pea-sized crumbles.

4   Slowly mix in milk until a dough forms.

5   Place dough on a clean, floured surface. Knead dough ten times until no longer sticky. Roll out dough to ¼" thick, adding flour as needed.

6   Use a biscuit cutter to cut out 2" rounds of dough.

7   Once there is no longer room to make additional cuts, roll dough back out and continue to cut until there are twelve biscuit rounds.

8   Working in batches, place biscuits, spaced ½" apart, inside air fryer.

9   Air fry 10 minutes. Serve.

PER SERVING (SERVING SIZE: 2 BISCUITS)

CALORIES: 283 | FAT: 9g | PROTEIN: 7g | SODIUM: 538mg | FIBER: 1g | CARBOHYDRATES: 43g | SUGAR: 2g

Smashed Red Potatoes

Prior to air frying, these tasty potatoes are boiled and then smashed down and coated in butter before getting mixed with cheese and bacon pieces. Top them with a dollop of sour cream, if desired.

Hands-On Time: 17 minutes
Cook Time: 24 minutes (per batch)
Total Recipe Cost: $2.77

Serves 4

- 4 medium red potatoes, halved
- 2 tablespoons unsalted butter, melted
- ½ teaspoon salt
- ¼ teaspoon ground black pepper
- ½ cup grated sharp Cheddar cheese
- 1 strip bacon, cooked and crumbled

1 On the stovetop, bring a large pot of salted water to a boil over high heat. Add potatoes to water and boil until fork-tender, about 12 minutes.

2 Preheat air fryer to 400°F.

3 Remove potatoes from water and place skin-side down on a rimmed cookie sheet. Use a potato masher to smash potatoes down until 1" thick.

4 Scoop smashed potatoes up with a spatula and place in a single layer inside air fryer (you may need to work in batches).

5 Brush top of potatoes with melted butter and season with salt and pepper. Sprinkle with cheese and bacon.

6 Air fry 12 minutes. Serve warm.

PER SERVING

CALORIES: 268 | FAT: 12g | PROTEIN: 7g | SODIUM: 797mg | FIBER: 3g | CARBOHYDRATES: 31g | SUGAR: 1g

Parmesan Cauliflower

You can have tasty cauliflower ready in just 20 minutes in your air fryer. I love this simple recipe with the salty flavor of Parmesan cheese. If you don't have avocado oil on hand, olive oil may be used.

Hands-On Time: 10 minutes
Cook Time: 20 minutes
Total Recipe Cost: $4.43

Serves 4

1 large head cauliflower, cut into florets
¼ cup avocado oil
1 teaspoon garlic salt
½ teaspoon ground black pepper
¼ cup grated Parmesan cheese

1 Preheat air fryer to 400°F.

2 In a medium bowl, combine cauliflower, oil, garlic salt, and pepper. Mix well.

3 Arrange cauliflower in a single layer inside air fryer.

4 Air fry 20 minutes, shaking or turning every 5 minutes.

5 Sprinkle with cheese, then serve.

PER SERVING

CALORIES: 199 | FAT: 15g | PROTEIN: 6g | SODIUM: 665mg | FIBER: 4g | CARBOHYDRATES: 11g | SUGAR: 4g

Garlic Toast

Skip the expensive loaf of garlic bread and make your own delicious Garlic Toast at home in your air fryer. This recipe uses sourdough bread, but any sliced bread will work.

Hands-On Time: 12 minutes
Cook Time: 5 minutes (per batch)
Total Recipe Cost: $1.01

Serves 4

- 2 tablespoons salted butter, softened
- 1 tablespoon minced garlic
- 1 teaspoon minced fresh flat-leaf Italian parsley
- 4 (½"-thick) slices sourdough bread

1 Preheat air fryer to 400°F.

2 In a small bowl, combine butter, garlic, and parsley. Spread butter mixture onto bread.

3 Place bread inside air fryer with the butter side up (you may need to work in batches).

4 Air fry 5 minutes until golden brown. Serve.

PER SERVING

CALORIES: 129 | FAT: 6g | PROTEIN: 3g | SODIUM: 139mg | FIBER: 1g | CARBOHYDRATES: 15g | SUGAR: 2g

Cheddar Drop Biscuits

Take your classic biscuits and add extra flavor with Cheddar and garlic! These drop biscuits cook up nicely in an air fryer.

Hands-On Time: 15 minutes
Cook Time: 10 minutes (per batch)
Total Recipe Cost: $2.84

Serves 6

2 cups all-purpose flour
1 cup shredded sharp
   Cheddar cheese
⅔ cup whole milk
½ cup unsalted butter,
   melted
1 large egg
2 tablespoons minced garlic
1 tablespoon baking powder
1 teaspoon salt

1 Preheat air fryer to 400°F.

2 In a large bowl, combine all ingredients and mix well.

3 Drop ¼-cup scoops of batter inside air fryer, spaced 1" apart.

4 Working in batches, air fry biscuits 10 minutes until golden brown. Serve.

PER SERVING (SERVING SIZE: 2 BISCUITS)

CALORIES: 397 | FAT: 22g | PROTEIN: 11g | SODIUM: 778mg | FIBER: 1g | CARBOHYDRATES: 35g | SUGAR: 2g

5

Chicken Main Dishes

Chicken is a staple in many frugal kitchens because it is so versatile and filling. This chapter will show you how to quickly whip together a chicken dish that is easy to make and tastes great. Many of these recipes are ready in 30 minutes or less. From Chicken Nuggets to Cajun Chicken Wings and Buttermilk Chicken Tenders to Chicken Fajitas, you are sure to find a recipe that fulfills your craving!

Lemon Pepper Chicken Wings

Chicken wings in the air fryer cook quickly and come out extra crispy on the outside. When shopping for this recipe, look for chicken wing sections. Frozen chicken tends to be less expensive than fresh chicken—unless the chicken is on sale.

Hands-On Time: 22 minutes
Cook Time: 30 minutes (per batch)
Total Recipe Cost: $5.83

Serves 5

2 tablespoons lemon zest
1½ teaspoons ground black pepper
1 teaspoon salt
1 teaspoon onion powder
½ teaspoon garlic powder
10 chicken wing sections (2 pounds total)
¼ cup olive oil

USING FROZEN WINGS

If using frozen wings, prepare as directed and add 10 minutes to the cook time and flip after 20 minutes.

1. Preheat air fryer to 380°F.

2. In a small bowl, combine lemon zest, pepper, salt, onion powder, and garlic powder.

3. Brush both sides of chicken with oil and rub with seasoning mixture.

4. Spray inside of air fryer with olive oil spray.

5. Arrange chicken wings in a single layer inside air fryer, spaced ½" apart to allow for air flow (you may need to work in batches).

6. Air fry 30 minutes, turning halfway through the cooking time, until crispy and chicken reaches an internal temperature of 165°F. Serve.

PER SERVING

CALORIES: 532 | FAT: 38g | PROTEIN: 41g | SODIUM: 632mg | FIBER: 1g | CARBOHYDRATES: 1g | SUGAR: 0g

Cajun Chicken Wings

Beware: These can be a bit spicy! If you are looking for flavors of the bayou without as much heat, try cutting back on the cayenne pepper.

Hands-On Time: 22 minutes
Cook Time: 30 minutes (per batch)
Total Recipe Cost: $6.08

Serves 5

- 1 teaspoon salt
- 1 teaspoon garlic powder
- 1 teaspoon paprika
- ¾ teaspoon dried oregano
- ¾ teaspoon dried thyme
- ½ teaspoon ground black pepper
- ½ teaspoon onion powder
- ½ teaspoon cayenne pepper
- ¼ teaspoon red pepper flakes
- 10 chicken wing sections (2 pounds total)
- ¼ cup olive oil

1 Preheat air fryer to 380°F.

2 In a small bowl, combine salt, garlic powder, paprika, oregano, thyme, black pepper, onion powder, cayenne pepper, and red pepper flakes.

3 Brush both sides of chicken with oil and rub with seasoning mixture.

4 Spray inside of air fryer with olive oil spray.

5 Arrange chicken wings in a single layer inside air fryer, spaced ½" apart to allow for air flow (you may need to work in batches).

6 Air fry 30 minutes, turning halfway through the cooking time, until crispy and chicken reaches an internal temperature of 165°F. Serve.

PER SERVING

CALORIES: 532 | FAT: 38g | PROTEIN: 41g | SODIUM: 632mg |
FIBER: 0g | CARBOHYDRATES: 1g | SUGAR: 0g

Chili Ranch Chicken Thighs

Chili Ranch Chicken Thighs have the perfect amount of spice and seasoning. They come out crispy on the outside and juicy on the inside—thanks to the air fryer. Be sure to use a meat thermometer when cooking this chicken, as bone-in chicken tends to take longer to cook.

Hands-On Time: 10 minutes
Cook Time: 30 minutes
Total Recipe Cost: $2.52

Serves 4

1 tablespoon olive oil
4 bone-in chicken thighs (1½ pounds total)
2 teaspoons ranch seasoning
1 teaspoon chili powder
½ teaspoon paprika
½ teaspoon salt
¼ teaspoon ground black pepper

MEAL PREPPING?

This chicken is great for meal prep. It can be made on Sunday night and eaten for several days. It tastes great when sliced and served over a simple salad.

1 Preheat air fryer to 400°F.

2 Brush oil over both sides of chicken.

3 In a small bowl, mix together ranch seasoning, chili powder, paprika, salt, and pepper.

4 Spray inside of air fryer with olive oil spray. Coat outside of chicken with seasoning mixture. Arrange chicken in a single layer inside air fryer, spaced ½" apart to allow for air flow.

5 Air fry 30 minutes, flipping halfway through the cooking time, until chicken reaches an internal temperature of 165°F. Serve.

PER SERVING

CALORIES: 355 | FAT: 22g | PROTEIN: 32g | SODIUM: 584mg | FIBER: 0g | CARBOHYDRATES: 2g | SUGAR: 0g

Pretzel-Crusted Chicken Strips

This recipe makes perfectly cooked chicken strips with an extra-crunchy pretzel coating! Make sure to coat the inside of your air fryer well with oil, as the pretzel coating tends to want to stick to the air fryer while cooking.

Hands-On Time: 15 minutes
Cook Time: 14 minutes
Total Recipe Cost: $7.71

Serves 4

2 cups mini pretzels
¾ cup panko bread crumbs
1 teaspoon garlic salt
½ teaspoon paprika
½ teaspoon Cajun seasoning
2 large eggs, beaten
8 boneless, skinless chicken tenders (1 pound total)

1 Preheat air fryer to 370°F. Line a cookie sheet with parchment paper and set aside.

2 Place pretzels in the bowl of a food processor and process until they reach the consistency of bread crumbs.

3 In a medium bowl, combine pretzel crumbs, bread crumbs, garlic salt, paprika, and Cajun seasoning.

4 Place eggs in a separate medium bowl.

5 Dip chicken in eggs and shake off any excess, then dip in pretzel coating.

6 Spray inside of air fryer with olive oil spray.

7 Arrange coated chicken inside air fryer, spaced ½" apart, and spray with olive oil spray.

8 Air fry 14 minutes, flipping halfway through the cooking time, until chicken reaches an internal temperature of 165°F. Serve warm.

PER SERVING

CALORIES: 344 | **FAT:** 4g | **PROTEIN:** 29g | **SODIUM:** 1,098mg | **FIBER:** 2g | **CARBOHYDRATES:** 46g | **SUGAR:** 2g

Chicken Taquitos

These air-fried taquitos come out super crispy with a flavorful filling. This is a great recipe for using up leftover cooked chicken, but leftover taco meat could also be used.

Hands-On Time: 25 minutes
Cook Time: 5 minutes
Total Recipe Cost: $6.24

Serves 4

- 2½ cups shredded cooked chicken (12 ounces total)
- 1 (4-ounce) can diced mild green chilies
- ½ cup shredded Mexican cheese blend
- 2 tablespoons taco seasoning
- 12 (6") corn tortillas

1 Preheat air fryer to 400°F.

2 In a large bowl, combine chicken, chilies, cheese, and taco seasoning.

3 Place ¼ cup chicken mixture on each tortilla and roll up tightly. Secure tortillas with a toothpick.

4 Arrange taquitos inside air fryer, spaced ½" apart, and spray with olive oil spray.

5 Air fry 5 minutes until crispy. Remove toothpicks prior to serving. Serve warm.

PER SERVING (SERVING SIZE: 3 TAQUITOS)

CALORIES: 403 | FAT: 9g | PROTEIN: 35g | SODIUM: 552mg | FIBER: 7g | CARBOHYDRATES: 43g | SUGAR: 2g

Buttermilk Chicken Tenders

The buttermilk in this recipe makes the chicken extra tender and juicy, while the panko coating adds that perfect crispy texture on the outside. These Buttermilk Chicken Tenders taste even better when paired with a dipping sauce like buttermilk ranch dressing.

Hands-On Time: 15 minutes
Cook Time: 14 minutes
Total Recipe Cost: $8.22

Serves 4

8 boneless, skinless chicken tenders (1 pound total)
1½ cups buttermilk
½ cup all-purpose flour
4 large eggs, beaten
1 cup panko bread crumbs
1 tablespoon seasoned salt
1 teaspoon paprika
1 teaspoon dried parsley
½ teaspoon ground black pepper

1 Place chicken in a shallow baking dish and cover with buttermilk. Let sit refrigerated 1 hour.

2 Preheat air fryer to 370°F. Line a cookie sheet with parchment paper and set aside.

3 Place flour in a medium shallow bowl. Place eggs in a second medium shallow bowl.

4 In a third medium shallow bowl, combine bread crumbs, seasoned salt, paprika, parsley, and pepper. Stir to combine.

5 Drain buttermilk from chicken.

6 Working in batches, dredge chicken in flour. Dip chicken in eggs, shaking off any excess, and then in bread crumbs.

7 Dip chicken in eggs again and dredge in bread crumbs a second time. Place coated chicken on prepared cookie sheet.

8 Spray inside of air fryer with olive oil spray.

9 Arrange chicken inside air fryer, spaced ½" apart. Spray chicken with olive oil spray.

10 Air fry 14 minutes, flipping halfway through the cooking time, until chicken reaches an internal temperature of 165°F. Serve warm.

PER SERVING

CALORIES: 284 | **FAT:** 5g | **PROTEIN:** 30g | **SODIUM:** 1,362mg | **FIBER:** 1g | **CARBOHYDRATES:** 27g | **SUGAR:** 2g

Chicken Parmesan

Now you can make this classic dish in the air fryer. This spin on the recipe features chicken that is coated in Parmesan cheese and topped with marinara sauce and more cheese. For a complete meal, serve this dish over a bed of spaghetti and paired with a green salad.

Hands-On Time: 20 minutes
Cook Time: 9 minutes
Total Recipe Cost: $6.54

Serves 4

1 teaspoon salt, divided
¼ teaspoon ground black pepper
2 (6-ounce) boneless, skinless chicken breasts, each butterflied into two equal pieces
¼ cup unsalted butter, melted
½ cup grated Parmesan cheese
1 tablespoon Italian seasoning
1 teaspoon garlic powder
½ cup marinara sauce
½ cup shredded mozzarella cheese

1 Preheat air fryer to 360°F.

2 Sprinkle ½ teaspoon salt and pepper on both sides of chicken.

3 Brush melted butter on both sides of chicken.

4 In a small bowl, combine Parmesan, Italian seasoning, garlic powder, and remaining ½ teaspoon salt. Mix well.

5 Dip chicken in cheese mixture so it is coated on both sides.

6 Place coated chicken inside air fryer, spaced ½" apart. Spray with olive oil spray.

7 Air fry 6 minutes. Then flip chicken over. Top with marinara sauce and mozzarella.

8 Air fry an additional 3 minutes until chicken reaches an internal temperature of 165°F. Serve warm.

PER SERVING

CALORIES: 299 | FAT: 18g | PROTEIN: 24g | SODIUM: 1,164mg | FIBER: 1g | CARBOHYDRATES: 6g | SUGAR: 2g

Whole Chicken

Air frying a whole chicken is a great way to save money because a whole chicken can be split into multiple meals and the bones can then be boiled in water to make chicken broth. When choosing a chicken, be sure to pick one that will fit inside your air fryer.

Hands-On Time: 30 minutes
Cook Time: 1 hour
Total Recipe Cost: $7.39

Serves 6

1 (5-pound) whole chicken
4 tablespoons avocado oil
2 teaspoons paprika
1 teaspoon salt
1 teaspoon dried sage
1 teaspoon onion powder
½ teaspoon garlic powder
¼ teaspoon cayenne pepper
¼ teaspoon ground black pepper

1 Preheat air fryer to 380°F.

2 Remove and discard giblets from chicken. Pat outside of chicken dry. Use cooking twine to tie legs and wings to chicken.

3 In a small bowl, mix together oil, paprika, salt, sage, onion powder, garlic powder, cayenne pepper, and black pepper.

4 Use a pastry brush to brush spice mixture all over chicken, including under wings and skin. Place chicken inside air fryer.

5 Air fry 30 minutes, then flip. Cook an additional 30 minutes until chicken reaches an internal temperature of 165°F.

PER SERVING

CALORIES: 510 | FAT: 34g | PROTEIN: 40g | SODIUM: 496mg | FIBER: 0g | CARBOHYDRATES: 1g | SUGAR: 0g

Spicy Hasselback Chicken

Similar to the popular potato recipe, this Spicy Hasselback Chicken features chicken breasts with slices partway through, which are loaded with cheese, jalapeños, and bacon.

Hands-On Time: 10 minutes
Cook Time: 16 minutes
Total Recipe Cost: $11.82

Serves 4

- 4 (6-ounce) boneless, skinless chicken breasts
- ¾ teaspoon salt
- ¼ teaspoon ground black pepper
- 8 ounces cream cheese, softened
- 2 medium jalapeños, seeded and diced
- 4 slices bacon, cooked and crumbled
- 2 medium green onions, sliced
- ½ cup shredded sharp Cheddar cheese
- ½ cup shredded mozzarella cheese

1 Preheat air fryer to 360°F.

2 Season chicken with salt and pepper.

3 Make slices in chicken ⅔ of the way down, ¼" apart. Don't slice all the way through.

4 In a medium bowl, mix together cream cheese, jalapeños, bacon, and green onions.

5 Stuff cream cheese mixture inside slits in chicken. Place prepared chicken inside air fryer.

6 Air fry 10 minutes, then top chicken with Cheddar and mozzarella.

7 Air fry an additional 6 minutes until chicken reaches an internal temperature of 165°F. Serve warm.

PER SERVING

CALORIES: 522 | FAT: 30g | PROTEIN: 50g | SODIUM: 1,256mg | FIBER: 0g | CARBOHYDRATES: 5g | SUGAR: 3g

Bruschetta Chicken

Bruschetta Chicken is a twist on the Italian appetizer. In this recipe, chicken is topped with a combination of fresh tomato, basil, and garlic and is finished with a drizzle of balsamic glaze.

Hands-On Time: 20 minutes
Cook Time: 12 minutes
Total Recipe Cost: $10.28

Serves 4

1 tablespoon Italian seasoning

1 teaspoon garlic powder

1½ teaspoons salt, divided

¼ teaspoon ground black pepper

¼ teaspoon onion powder

⅛ teaspoon red pepper flakes

2 (6-ounce) boneless, skinless chicken breasts, each butterflied into two equal pieces

3 medium Roma tomatoes, diced

4 tablespoons chopped fresh basil

2 tablespoons minced garlic

2 tablespoons extra-virgin olive oil

½ cup shaved Parmesan cheese

¼ cup balsamic glaze

1 Preheat air fryer to 360°F.

2 In a small bowl, mix together Italian seasoning, garlic powder, 1 teaspoon salt, black pepper, onion powder, and red pepper flakes.

3 Rub seasoning all over chicken. Place chicken inside air fryer.

4 Air fry 12 minutes, flipping halfway through the cooking time, until chicken reaches an internal temperature of 165°F.

5 While chicken is cooking, combine tomatoes, basil, garlic, oil, and remaining ½ teaspoon salt in a medium bowl.

6 Top chicken with tomato mixture and then cheese. Drizzle with balsamic glaze, then serve.

PER SERVING

CALORIES: 275 | FAT: 12g | PROTEIN: 23g | SODIUM: 1,232mg | FIBER: 2g | CARBOHYDRATES: 22g | SUGAR: 18g

DON'T HAVE FRESH TOMATOES AND BASIL?

If you don't have any fresh tomatoes, you can substitute with 1 (15-ounce) can of diced tomatoes. Fresh basil may be substituted with 1 tablespoon dried basil.

Pesto Chicken

If you love pesto, you will love this Pesto Chicken recipe! It cooks quickly and perfectly in the air fryer and is topped with pesto, melted cheese, and sliced tomato.

Hands-On Time: 20 minutes
Cook Time: 12 minutes
Total Recipe Cost: $5.88

Serves 4

- 1 tablespoon Italian seasoning
- 1 teaspoon garlic powder
- 1 teaspoon salt
- ½ teaspoon ground black pepper
- 2 (6-ounce) boneless, skinless chicken breasts, each butterflied into two equal pieces
- ½ cup basil pesto
- ½ cup shredded mozzarella cheese
- 1 large tomato, cut into four slices

1 Preheat air fryer to 360°F.

2 In a small bowl, mix Italian seasoning, garlic powder, salt, and pepper. Rub seasoning mixture over both sides of chicken.

3 Place chicken inside air fryer. Air fry 5 minutes.

4 Flip chicken over inside air fryer, then spread pesto over chicken and top with cheese and tomato slices.

5 Air fry an additional 7 minutes until chicken reaches an internal temperature of 165°F. Serve.

PER SERVING

CALORIES: 263 | **FAT:** 16g | **PROTEIN:** 24g | **SODIUM:** 1,091mg | **FIBER:** 1g | **CARBOHYDRATES:** 6g | **SUGAR:** 3g

Bacon-Wrapped Chicken

This chicken is going to be your go-to fancy dish! The combination of brown sugar and bacon makes for a flavor-packed meal you will make again and again. When selecting bacon for this dish, make sure it is not thick-cut bacon, as it will not cook at the same rate as the chicken.

Hands-On Time: 25 minutes
Cook Time: 12 minutes
Total Recipe Cost: $6.15

Serves 4

- ¼ cup packed light brown sugar
- 2 teaspoons paprika
- ½ teaspoon salt
- ¼ teaspoon ground black pepper
- ¼ teaspoon onion powder
- 2 (6-ounce) boneless, skinless chicken breasts, each butterflied into two equal pieces
- 8 slices bacon

1 Preheat air fryer to 360°F.

2 In a small bowl, mix together brown sugar, paprika, salt, pepper, and onion powder. Rub seasoning mixture over both sides of chicken.

3 Wrap each piece of chicken with 2 bacon slices and secure with a toothpick. Place chicken inside air fryer.

4 Air fry 12 minutes, flipping halfway through the cooking time, until chicken reaches an internal temperature of 165°F. Remove toothpicks prior to serving.

PER SERVING

CALORIES: 232 | FAT: 8g | PROTEIN: 25g | SODIUM: 750mg | FIBER: 0g | CARBOHYDRATES: 14g | SUGAR: 13g

Spinach-Stuffed Chicken

Chicken stuffed with a combination of cream cheese, Parmesan cheese, and spinach makes for a deliciously creamy meal. Be careful not to slice the chicken completely in half when cutting the pocket. You want the filling to be stuffed inside the chicken, not falling out the other end.

Hands-On Time: 25 minutes
Cook Time: 16 minutes
Total Recipe Cost: $9.81

Serves 4

4 (6-ounce) boneless, skinless chicken breasts
1 teaspoon paprika
1½ teaspoons salt, divided
¼ teaspoon garlic powder
¼ teaspoon onion powder
4 ounces cream cheese, softened
½ cup grated Parmesan cheese
1 cup chopped baby spinach
2 tablespoons mayonnaise
1 teaspoon minced garlic
½ teaspoon red pepper flakes

SOFTENED CREAM CHEESE

It is important for the cream cheese to be fully softened prior to mixing, or it will be very difficult to mix with the other ingredients. The best way to do this is to take the cream cheese out of the refrigerator an hour before you plan to start cooking.

1 Preheat air fryer to 360°F.

2 Cut a pocket in the side of each chicken breast that is just less than the length and width of chicken.

3 In a small bowl, mix together paprika, 1 teaspoon salt, garlic powder, and onion powder. Rub seasoning mixture all over chicken.

4 In a medium bowl, mix together cream cheese, Parmesan, spinach, mayonnaise, garlic, red pepper flakes, and remaining ½ teaspoon salt.

5 Use a spoon to stuff cheese mixture in each chicken breast. Place chicken inside air fryer.

6 Air fry 16 minutes until chicken reaches an internal temperature of 165°F. Serve warm.

PER SERVING

CALORIES: 382 | FAT: 21g | PROTEIN: 42g | SODIUM: 1,514mg | FIBER: 0g | CARBOHYDRATES: 4g | SUGAR: 1g

Broccoli Chicken Casserole

Air fryers are great for making small batches of casseroles. This Broccoli Chicken Casserole is a combination of leftover chicken, rice, broccoli, and a creamy sauce.

Hands-On Time: 10 minutes
Cook Time: 20 minutes
Total Recipe Cost: $9.46

Serves 4

2 cups diced cooked chicken (10 ounces total)
1½ cups cooked white rice
2 cups frozen broccoli florets, defrosted
2 cups shredded sharp Cheddar cheese, divided
1 (10.5-ounce) can cream of chicken soup
½ cup whole milk
½ cup sour cream
1 teaspoon Italian seasoning
½ teaspoon salt
¼ teaspoon ground black pepper

1 Preheat air fryer to 320°F.

2 In a nonstick baking dish that fits inside your air fryer, combine chicken, rice, broccoli, 1½ cups cheese, soup, milk, sour cream, Italian seasoning, salt, and pepper. Mix well.

3 Place dish inside air fryer. Air fry 15 minutes, then top casserole with remaining ½ cup cheese and air fry an additional 5 minutes until melted and golden brown. Serve.

PER SERVING

CALORIES: 607 | **FAT:** 30g | **PROTEIN:** 42g | **SODIUM:** 1,215mg | **FIBER:** 6g | **CARBOHYDRATES:** 31g | **SUGAR:** 4g

WHAT KIND OF RICE SHOULD YOU USE?

Any variety of leftover cooked rice may be used in this recipe. Keep in mind that the flavor of the rice will carry over into the dish. So, if your family is used to the flavor and consistency of white rice, then you should stick with that variety.

Orange Chicken

This Chinese takeout copycat dish has the best-tasting sauce with tender chunks of chicken. It's important to cook this dish in a cake pan. Otherwise, the yummy orange sauce will slide right off the chicken and into the bottom of your air fryer.

Hands-On Time: 20 minutes
Cook Time: 30 minutes
Total Recipe Cost: $4.09

Serves 4

2 large eggs, beaten
1 cup all-purpose flour
1 teaspoon salt
½ teaspoon ground black pepper
2 (6-ounce) boneless, skinless chicken breasts, cut into 1" pieces
½ cup orange juice
½ cup granulated sugar
¼ cup low-sodium soy sauce
2 tablespoons packed light brown sugar
1 tablespoon sriracha
2 teaspoons minced garlic
2 teaspoons ginger paste
2 teaspoons rice wine vinegar
½ teaspoon red pepper flakes

1 Preheat air fryer to 350°F. Spray a 7" cake pan with olive oil spray and set aside.

2 Place eggs in a medium shallow bowl. In a second medium shallow bowl, mix together flour, salt, and black pepper.

3 Dip chicken pieces into eggs and shake to remove any excess egg. Then, dip chicken into flour mixture. Place coated chicken in prepared pan.

4 In a small bowl, whisk together orange juice, granulated sugar, soy sauce, brown sugar, sriracha, garlic, ginger paste, vinegar, and red pepper flakes.

5 Pour sauce over chicken and gently stir to mix. Place pan inside air fryer.

6 Air fry 30 minutes, stirring every 10 minutes during the cooking time. Chicken is done when it reaches an internal temperature of 165°F. Serve warm.

PER SERVING

CALORIES: 323 | **FAT:** 3g | **PROTEIN:** 23g | **SODIUM:** 936mg | **FIBER:** 1g | **CARBOHYDRATES:** 51g | **SUGAR:** 36g

Chicken Nuggets

Make your own Chicken Nuggets at home and enjoy the extra flavor. Hot sauce is included in the ingredients but does not add much spice, just flavor. Be sure not to use extra-hot hot sauce unless you want spicy nuggets.

Hands-On Time: 25 minutes
Cook Time: 7 minutes
Total Recipe Cost: $8.47

Serves 6

2 cups buttermilk
1 tablespoon hot sauce
4 (6-ounce) boneless, skinless chicken breasts cut into 1" chunks
1 cup all-purpose flour
1 tablespoon garlic powder
2 teaspoons paprika
1½ teaspoons salt
1 teaspoon ground black pepper
2 large eggs, beaten
1 cup panko bread crumbs

1 In a shallow baking dish, mix together buttermilk and hot sauce.

2 Place chicken in buttermilk mixture and let soak a minimum of 30 minutes in refrigerator.

3 In a medium shallow bowl, mix together flour, garlic powder, paprika, salt, and pepper.

4 Place eggs in a second medium shallow bowl. Place bread crumbs in a third medium shallow bowl.

5 Preheat air fryer to 360°F.

6 Remove chicken from buttermilk mixture. Dredge chicken in flour mixture, turning to coat. Then dip chicken in eggs, shaking to remove any excess. Finally, dip chicken in bread crumbs, turning to evenly coat.

7 Spray inside of air fryer with olive oil spray.

8 Arrange chicken in an even layer inside air fryer, spaced ½" apart. Spray top of chicken with olive oil spray.

9 Air fry 7 minutes until chicken reaches an internal temperature of 165°F. Serve.

PER SERVING

CALORIES: 229 | FAT: 4g | PROTEIN: 28g | SODIUM: 522mg | FIBER: 1g | CARBOHYDRATES: 19g | SUGAR: 1g

Chicken Schnitzel

Schnitzel is traditionally a fried dish in which meat is beaten into a thin layer to tenderize it. This recipe follows the same steps, but instead of frying the meat in oil, it uses the air fryer. If you don't have a meat mallet, a rolling pin may be used to pound the chicken.

Hands-On Time: 20 minutes
Cook Time: 12 minutes
Total Recipe Cost: $8.00

Serves 4

4 (6-ounce) boneless, skinless chicken breasts
1 cup all-purpose flour
1 tablespoon garlic powder
2 teaspoons paprika
1½ teaspoons salt
1 teaspoon ground black pepper
2 large eggs
1 tablespoon Dijon mustard
1 cup panko bread crumbs
1 medium lemon, cut into wedges

1 Preheat air fryer to 360°F.

2 Cover chicken with parchment paper and use a meat mallet to beat chicken until it is thinned to ⅛" thick.

3 In a medium shallow bowl, mix together flour, garlic powder, paprika, salt, and pepper. Place eggs and mustard in a second medium shallow bowl and whisk until eggs are well beaten. Place bread crumbs in a third medium shallow bowl.

4 Dredge chicken in flour mixture, turning to coat. Next, dip chicken in egg mixture, shaking off any excess. Finally, dip chicken in bread crumbs.

5 Spray inside of air fryer with olive oil spray.

6 Place chicken inside air fryer in a single layer and spray chicken with olive oil spray.

7 Air fry 12 minutes, flipping halfway through the cooking time, until chicken reaches an internal temperature of 165°F.

8 Squeeze lemon juice over chicken prior to serving.

PER SERVING

CALORIES: 340 | FAT: 6g | PROTEIN: 42g | SODIUM: 806mg | FIBER: 1g | CARBOHYDRATES: 29g | SUGAR: 1g

Chicken Fajitas

Chicken Fajitas in the air fryer come out with perfectly tender peppers and juicy chicken. This recipe can be cooked ahead of time and used as an easy grab-and-go lunch. It can be stored in the refrigerator up to 3 days.

Hands-On Time: 15 minutes
Cook Time: 10 minutes
Total Recipe Cost: $7.64

Serves 4

2 (8-ounce) boneless, skinless chicken breasts, butterflied and cut into 2" strips

1 large red bell pepper, seeded and cut into 2"-long strips

½ large yellow onion, peeled and sliced

¼ cup taco seasoning

2 tablespoons olive oil

8 (6") flour tortillas, warmed

1 Preheat air fryer to 400°F.

2 In a large bowl, mix together chicken, bell pepper, onion, taco seasoning, and oil.

3 Place chicken mixture inside air fryer.

4 Air fry 10 minutes, stirring halfway through the cooking time. Chicken is done when it reaches an internal temperature of 165°F.

5 Serve on warm tortillas.

PER SERVING

CALORIES: 403 | **FAT:** 13g | **PROTEIN:** 30g | **SODIUM:** 1,218mg | **FIBER:** 4g | **CARBOHYDRATES:** 40g | **SUGAR:** 5g

Teriyaki Drumsticks

This recipe is simple but does take some time for marinating. Make sure to plan ahead and give yourself an extra 30 minutes so the chicken has time to marinate.

Hands-On Time: 15 minutes
Cook Time: 40 minutes
Total Recipe Cost: $6.70

Serves 6

6 chicken drumsticks
   (1½ pounds total)
2 cups teriyaki sauce, divided
½ cup unsalted butter,
   melted
1 medium green onion, sliced

1 Place chicken in a shallow baking dish.

2 Pour 1½ cups teriyaki sauce over chicken and refrigerate a minimum of 30 minutes and up to 8 hours.

3 Preheat air fryer to 370°F.

4 Remove chicken from teriyaki sauce and discard sauce. Brush melted butter on chicken.

5 Arrange chicken inside air fryer without overcrowding.

6 Air fry 35 minutes, then brush remaining ½ cup teriyaki sauce over chicken and air fry an additional 5 minutes. Chicken is done when it reaches an internal temperature of 165°F.

7 Serve chicken garnished with green onion.

PER SERVING

CALORIES: 335 | FAT: 21g | PROTEIN: 24g | SODIUM: 1,471mg | FIBER: 0g | CARBOHYDRATES: 6g | SUGAR: 5g

Barbecue Drumsticks

These drumsticks will take on the flavor of the barbecue sauce you choose. Make sure to select a barbecue sauce you regularly use and enjoy.

Hands-On Time: 15 minutes
Cook Time: 40 minutes
Total Recipe Cost: $5.22

Serves 6

6 chicken drumsticks
   (1½ pounds total)
½ teaspoon salt
¼ teaspoon ground black
   pepper
½ cup unsalted butter,
   melted
1 cup barbecue sauce
2 tablespoons minced fresh
   parsley

1 Preheat air fryer to 370°F.

2 Pat chicken dry and season with salt and pepper, then brush melted butter over chicken.

3 Arrange chicken inside air fryer without overcrowding.

4 Air fry 30 minutes, then brush barbecue sauce all over chicken. Air fry an additional 10 minutes. Chicken is done when it reaches an internal temperature of 165°F.

5 Serve garnished with parsley.

PER SERVING

CALORIES: 385 | FAT: 22g | PROTEIN: 22g | SODIUM: 775mg | FIBER: 1g | CARBOHYDRATES: 20g | SUGAR: 16g

Buffalo Drumsticks

Spicy buffalo sauce on chicken drumsticks is the perfect combination. The chicken comes out crispy on the outside, and the sauce gets nice and sticky in the air fryer.

Hands-On Time: 15 minutes
Cook Time: 40 minutes
Total Recipe Cost: $6.74

Serves 6

6 chicken drumsticks
    (1½ pounds total)
½ teaspoon salt
¼ teaspoon ground black
    pepper
½ cup unsalted butter,
    melted
1 cup buffalo sauce
2 tablespoons ranch
    seasoning

MAKE YOUR OWN BUFFALO SAUCE

Make your own buffalo sauce with ¾ cup hot sauce, ¼ cup butter, and 2 tablespoons red wine vinegar. Whisk together and use in place of store-bought buffalo sauce.

1   Preheat air fryer to 370°F.

2   Pat chicken dry and season with salt and pepper, then brush melted butter over chicken.

3   Arrange drumsticks inside air fryer without overcrowding. Air fry 30 minutes.

4   In a small bowl, whisk together buffalo sauce and ranch seasoning. Brush sauce mixture all over chicken.

5   Air fry an additional 10 minutes. Chicken is done when it reaches an internal temperature of 165°F. Serve.

PER SERVING

CALORIES: 312 | **FAT:** 21g | **PROTEIN:** 22g | **SODIUM:** 1,781mg | **FIBER:** 0g | **CARBOHYDRATES:** 2g | **SUGAR:** 0g

Honey Garlic Chicken

Using honey and garlic in this chicken recipe gives you the combination of sweet and savory in a delicious sauce. Serve it over rice with steamed broccoli for a complete meal.

Hands-On Time: 20 minutes
Cook Time: 30 minutes
Total Recipe Cost: $4.87

Serves 4

2 large eggs, beaten
1 cup all-purpose flour
1 teaspoon salt
1 teaspoon garlic powder
½ teaspoon ground black pepper
2 (6-ounce) boneless, skinless chicken breasts, cut into 1" pieces
¼ cup honey
¼ cup rice wine vinegar
3 tablespoons minced garlic
2 tablespoons low-sodium soy sauce
1 teaspoon red pepper flakes

1 Preheat air fryer to 350°F. Spray a 7" cake pan with olive oil spray and set aside.

2 Place eggs in a medium shallow bowl. In a second medium shallow bowl, mix together flour, salt, garlic powder, and black pepper.

3 Dip chicken pieces in eggs and then in flour mixture. Place coated chicken in prepared pan.

4 In a small bowl, whisk together honey, vinegar, minced garlic, soy sauce, and red pepper flakes. Pour sauce over chicken and gently stir.

5 Place pan inside air fryer and air fry 30 minutes, stirring every 10 minutes. Chicken is done when it reaches an internal temperature of 165°F. Serve warm.

PER SERVING

CALORIES: 313 | FAT: 3g | PROTEIN: 22g | SODIUM: 659mg | FIBER: 1g | CARBOHYDRATES: 51g | SUGAR: 35g

6

Beef and Pork Main Dishes

There are so many great dishes you can make in your air fryer with beef or pork as the star. To save money on these recipes, make sure to check your weekly grocery flyers for deals before buying meat. Make sure to freeze the meat well by either using a vacuum sealer or wrapping meat in freezer paper before placing in a freezer-safe bag. Some of the recipes you will make in this chapter are Bacon Cheddar Burgers, Beef Empanadas, and Brown Sugar Pork Chops.

Blue Cheese Burgers

These tasty burgers are made with ground beef, green onions, and blue cheese. They are zesty burgers packed with flavor.

Hands-On Time: 20 minutes
Cook Time: 8 minutes
Total Recipe Cost: $7.97

Serves 4

- 1 pound (93% lean) ground beef
- ½ cup crumbled blue cheese
- 2 medium green onions, sliced
- 1 large egg
- 1 tablespoon Dijon mustard
- 1 teaspoon minced garlic
- 1 teaspoon salt
- ¼ teaspoon ground black pepper
- 4 hamburger buns
- 4 leaves romaine lettuce
- 4 slices tomato

1 Preheat air fryer to 370°F.

2 In a medium bowl, combine ground beef, cheese, onions, egg, mustard, garlic, salt, and pepper. Mix well.

3 Divide meat into four equal pieces and shape each into a ½"-thick burger.

4 Spray inside of air fryer with olive oil spray. Arrange burgers inside air fryer ½" apart.

5 Air fry 8 minutes, flipping halfway through the cooking time.

6 Serve burgers on buns topped with lettuce and tomato.

PER SERVING

CALORIES: 363 | **FAT:** 14g | **PROTEIN:** 32g | **SODIUM:** 1,148mg | **FIBER:** 2g | **CARBOHYDRATES:** 24g | **SUGAR:** 4g

Meatloaf

This air fryer Meatloaf is juicy on the inside and crispy on the outside. Plus, making it in an air fryer is faster than the oven! You are going to love this classic recipe made new in the air fryer.

Hands-On Time: 20 minutes
Cook Time: 30 minutes
Total Recipe Cost: $5.19

Serves 4

1 pound (93% lean) ground beef
½ cup ketchup, divided
½ cup bread crumbs
¼ cup diced yellow onion
¼ cup whole milk
2 large eggs
2 medium cloves garlic, peeled and minced
2 tablespoons Worcestershire sauce
1 tablespoon Italian seasoning
1 teaspoon salt
½ teaspoon ground black pepper

1 Preheat air fryer to 330°F.

2 In a large bowl, combine all ingredients except ¼ cup ketchup. Mix well until fully combined.

3 Form mixture into a loaf and place inside air fryer.

4 Air fry 30 minutes. Brush remaining ¼ cup ketchup on top during last 5 minutes of cooking.

5 Let rest 10 minutes before serving.

PER SERVING

CALORIES: 291 | FAT: 9g | PROTEIN: 28g | SODIUM: 1,125mg | FIBER: 1g | CARBOHYDRATES: 22g | SUGAR: 9g

Meatloaf Muffins

Meatloaf Muffins are a tasty way to enjoy delicious meatloaf with extra-crispy tops. If you want to add a little sweetness, top the muffins with ketchup during the last 2 minutes of air frying.

Hands-On Time: 25 minutes
Cook Time: 16 minutes (per batch)
Total Recipe Cost: $6.08

Serves 6

½ pound (93% lean) ground beef
½ pound mild Italian sausage
½ cup bread crumbs
¼ cup diced yellow onion
¼ cup sour cream
¼ cup ketchup
2 large eggs
2 tablespoons Worcestershire sauce
1 tablespoon Italian seasoning
1 tablespoon minced garlic
1 teaspoon salt
1 teaspoon red pepper flakes
½ teaspoon ground black pepper

1 Preheat air fryer to 400°F. Grease a six-hole silicone egg mold and set aside.

2 In a medium bowl, combine all ingredients and mix well.

3 Scoop half of beef mixture into prepared egg mold and place inside air fryer.

4 Air fry 16 minutes. Serve warm.

5 Repeat with remaining beef mixture.

PER SERVING (SERVING SIZE: 2 MUFFINS)

CALORIES: 277 | FAT: 17g | PROTEIN: 17g | SODIUM: 920mg | FIBER: 1g | CARBOHYDRATES: 12g | SUGAR: 4g

MAKING A DOUBLE BATCH?
You can double or even triple this Meatloaf Muffins recipe and store the extras in your freezer for up to 3 months. When you're ready to eat them, reheat in your air fryer at 300°F until they reach an internal temperature of 160°F.

Brown Sugar Pork Chops

Pork chops taste great when paired with something sweet like this brown sugar rub. For an easy side dish, serve them with applesauce or Apple Chips (see recipe in Chapter 3).

Hands-On Time: 10 minutes
Cook Time: 9 minutes
Total Recipe Cost: $6.31

Serves 4

¼ cup packed light brown sugar
½ teaspoon cayenne pepper
½ teaspoon garlic powder
½ teaspoon paprika
½ teaspoon salt
¼ teaspoon ground black pepper
4 (4-ounce) thick-cut bone-in pork chops

1 Preheat air fryer to 370°F.

2 In a small bowl, mix together brown sugar, cayenne pepper, garlic powder, paprika, salt, and black pepper. Rub seasoning on both sides of pork chops.

3 Place pork chops in a single layer inside air fryer. Air fry 9 minutes, flipping halfway through the cooking time. Serve.

PER SERVING

CALORIES: 189 | FAT: 4g | PROTEIN: 25g | SODIUM: 369mg | FIBER: 0g | CARBOHYDRATES: 14g | SUGAR: 13g

Steak Tips

This dish is best served with a creamy side like mashed potatoes or creamed corn. Using sirloin steak is a great way to ensure a pricier cut of meat while still staying within your budget.

Hands-On Time: 10 minutes
Cook Time: 7 minutes
Total Recipe Cost: $7.50

Serves 4

1 teaspoon salt
1 teaspoon garlic powder
1 teaspoon paprika
½ teaspoon ground black pepper
½ teaspoon ground thyme
2 tablespoons olive oil
1 pound sirloin steak, cut into 1" pieces

1 Preheat air fryer to 400°F.

2 Sprinkle salt, garlic powder, paprika, pepper, thyme, and oil over steak. Toss to evenly coat steak in seasoning. Place steak inside air fryer.

3 Air fry 7 minutes, flipping halfway through the cooking time. Serve.

PER SERVING

CALORIES: 297 | FAT: 19g | PROTEIN: 25g | SODIUM: 630mg | FIBER: 0g | CARBOHYDRATES: 1g | SUGAR: 0g

Beef and Broccoli

Beef and Broccoli is a popular dish at many restaurants serving Chinese food. You can enjoy it at home at a fraction of the cost with this easy recipe.

Hands-On Time: 15 minutes
Cook Time: 17 minutes
Total Recipe Cost: $11.90

Serves 4

- 1 pound flank steak, sliced into ½"-wide strips
- ¼ cup cornstarch
- 1¼ teaspoons salt, divided
- ¼ teaspoon ground black pepper
- 1 cup beef broth
- 2 tablespoons minced garlic
- 1 tablespoon minced ginger
- 1 tablespoon honey
- 1 teaspoon sesame oil
- ¼ teaspoon red pepper flakes
- 4 cups broccoli florets
- 2 tablespoons olive oil
- 1 tablespoon sesame seeds

1 Preheat air fryer to 400°F.

2 In a medium bowl, combine steak, cornstarch, ¾ teaspoon salt, and black pepper. Mix to evenly coat steak.

3 In a small bowl, whisk together broth, garlic, ginger, honey, sesame oil, and red pepper flakes.

4 Place steak in a 7" cake pan. Pour sauce over steak and stir. Place pan inside air fryer.

5 Air fry 10 minutes, stirring halfway through the cooking time. Remove pan from air fryer and set aside.

6 Place broccoli inside air fryer. Drizzle with olive oil and remaining ½ teaspoon salt. Stir.

7 Air fry 7 minutes, shaking or turning halfway through the cooking time.

8 Combine steak with broccoli and top with sesame seeds. Serve warm.

PER SERVING

CALORIES: 355 | FAT: 16g | PROTEIN: 29g | SODIUM: 1,029mg | FIBER: 3g | CARBOHYDRATES: 20g | SUGAR: 6g

Mongolian Beef

Mongolian Beef is thin steak cooked in a rich sauce of brown sugar, soy sauce, and ginger. It tastes great served over sticky white rice.

Hands-On Time: 15 minutes
Cook Time: 10 minutes
Total Recipe Cost: $8.22

Serves 4

1 pound flank steak, sliced into thin strips
¼ cup cornstarch
1 teaspoon salt
¼ teaspoon ground black pepper
½ cup low-sodium soy sauce
½ cup packed light brown sugar
1 tablespoon minced garlic
2 teaspoons vegetable oil
½ teaspoon ginger paste
1 medium green onion, sliced

WHERE TO FIND GINGER PASTE
Ginger paste can often be found in the herb section of your grocery store. It usually comes in a clear tube. If you can't find ginger paste, fresh minced ginger may be used as a substitute.

1 Preheat air fryer to 400°F.

2 In a medium bowl, combine steak, cornstarch, salt, and pepper. Mix to evenly coat steak.

3 In a small bowl, whisk together soy sauce, brown sugar, garlic, oil, and ginger paste.

4 Place steak in a 7" cake pan. Pour sauce over steak and stir.

5 Air fry 10 minutes, stirring halfway through the cooking time.

6 Serve topped with green onion.

PER SERVING

CALORIES: 371 | FAT: 10g | PROTEIN: 28g | SODIUM: 1,476mg | FIBER: 0g | CARBOHYDRATES: 40g | SUGAR: 29g

Bacon Cheddar Burgers

What's better than a juicy burger? A juicy burger filled with bacon and Cheddar cheese. Skip the burger joint and make your own delicious burgers at home for less money and all of the flavor!

Hands-On Time: 20 minutes
Cook Time: 8 minutes
Total Recipe Cost: $8.73

Serves 4

1 pound (93% lean) ground beef
6 slices bacon, cooked and chopped
½ cup shredded sharp Cheddar cheese
1 large egg
1 tablespoon Worcestershire sauce
1 teaspoon salt
¼ teaspoon ground black pepper
4 hamburger buns
4 leaves romaine lettuce
4 slices tomato

1 Preheat air fryer to 370°F.

2 In a medium bowl, combine ground beef, bacon, cheese, egg, Worcestershire sauce, salt, and pepper. Mix well.

3 Divide meat into four equal pieces and shape each into a ½"-thick burger.

4 Spray inside of air fryer with olive oil spray. Arrange burgers inside air fryer, ½" apart.

5 Air fry 8 minutes, flipping halfway through the cooking time.

6 Serve burgers on buns with lettuce and tomato.

PER SERVING

CALORIES: 418 | FAT: 17g | PROTEIN: 37g | SODIUM: 1,235mg | FIBER: 2g | CARBOHYDRATES: 24g | SUGAR: 4g

Taco Casserole

Taco Casserole is beef nachos in casserole form. Serve it topped with sour cream and your favorite salsa. This casserole can be prepared ahead of time and stored in the freezer for up to 3 months. When ready to cook, defrost overnight in the refrigerator and air fry as directed.

Hands-On Time: 15 minutes
Cook Time: 4 minutes
Total Recipe Cost: $8.63

Serves 4

1 pound (93% lean) cooked ground beef
¼ cup taco seasoning
1½ cups crushed tortilla chips, divided
1 cup shredded Mexican cheese blend, divided
½ cup sour cream
½ cup salsa

1 Preheat air fryer to 400°F.

2 In a medium bowl, mix together ground beef and taco seasoning.

3 Spread half of beef mixture in a 7" cake pan. Top with ¾ cup tortilla chips and ½ cup cheese. Repeat with remaining beef, chips, and cheese.

4 Place pan inside air fryer. Air fry 4 minutes until cheese is melted and golden brown.

5 Serve topped with sour cream and salsa.

PER SERVING

CALORIES: 446 | FAT: 23g | PROTEIN: 31g | SODIUM: 1,067mg | FIBER: 3g | CARBOHYDRATES: 23g | SUGAR: 4g

Beef Empanadas

Empanadas are crescent-shaped pastries filled with a savory mixture of meat and vegetables. These Beef Empanadas take a bit of time to prepare, but the flavor is well worth the effort! Puff pastry can be found in the freezer section of your grocery store.

Hands-On Time: 25 minutes
Cook Time: 18 minutes (per batch)
Total Recipe Cost: $11.11

Serves 6

- 1 pound (93% lean) ground beef
- ½ cup chopped yellow onion
- ¼ cup beef broth
- 1 tablespoon minced garlic
- 1 tablespoon sriracha
- 2 teaspoons packed light brown sugar
- ½ teaspoon paprika
- ½ teaspoon chili powder
- ½ teaspoon salt
- ¼ teaspoon ground black pepper
- 3 sheets frozen puff pastry, thawed

1 Preheat air fryer to 400°F.

2 Mix ground beef and onion in 7" cake pan and place inside air fryer.

3 Air fry 10 minutes, stirring halfway through the cooking time. Drain fat from pan.

4 Top beef with broth, garlic, sriracha, brown sugar, paprika, chili powder, salt, and pepper. Stir well to combine.

5 Place pan back inside air fryer and air fry 3 minutes. Remove pan from air fryer and set aside.

6 Roll out puff pastry and cut each sheet into eight squares.

7 Place 1 tablespoon beef mixture on each pastry square. Fold each square in half (into a triangle) and use a fork to crimp edges.

8 Spray inside of air fryer with olive oil spray. Working in batches, arrange empanadas in a single layer inside air fryer. Spray top of empanadas with oil.

9 Air fry 5 minutes. Serve.

PER SERVING (SERVING SIZE: 4 EMPANADAS)

CALORIES: 800 | FAT: 49g | PROTEIN: 24g | SODIUM: 630mg | FIBER: 2g | CARBOHYDRATES: 60g | SUGAR: 4g

Beef and Rice–Stuffed Peppers

Stuffed peppers are a great way to enjoy a complete meal in one dish. Make sure to use cooked rice in this recipe, as rice will not cook at the same rate as the beef and bell peppers.

Hands-On Time: 15 minutes
Cook Time: 15 minutes
Total Recipe Cost: $7.08

Serves 4

1 pound (93% lean) ground beef
½ cup cooked white rice
1 cup tomato sauce
1 tablespoon Worcestershire sauce
1 tablespoon Italian seasoning
1 teaspoon garlic salt
½ teaspoon onion powder
⅛ teaspoon ground black pepper
4 medium red bell peppers, tops and seeds removed

1 Preheat air fryer to 350°F.

2 In a large bowl, combine ground beef, rice, tomato sauce, Worcestershire sauce, Italian seasoning, garlic salt, onion powder, and black pepper. Mix until fully combined.

3 Stuff beef mixture into bell peppers.

4 Carefully place bell peppers inside air fryer, standing up so filling does not fall out.

5 Air fry 15 minutes. Serve warm.

PER SERVING

CALORIES: 235 | FAT: 6g | PROTEIN: 25g | SODIUM: 874mg | FIBER: 4g | CARBOHYDRATES: 18g | SUGAR: 8g

Swedish Meatballs

Swedish Meatballs are tender meatballs made with ground beef and pork. They're served with a rich gravy that cooks on the stove as the meatballs cook in the air fryer.

Hands-On Time: 20 minutes
Cook Time: 15 minutes
Total Recipe Cost: $10.54

Serves 4

½ pound (93% lean) ground beef
½ pound ground pork
¼ cup diced yellow onion
¼ cup whole milk
¼ cup bread crumbs
1 large egg yolk
1½ teaspoons salt, divided
½ teaspoon ground black pepper, divided
⅛ teaspoon allspice
⅛ teaspoon ground nutmeg
¼ cup unsalted butter
¼ cup all-purpose flour
2 cups beef broth
½ cup sour cream
1 cup lingonberry sauce

1 Preheat air fryer to 360°F.

2 In a large bowl, combine ground beef, ground pork, onion, milk, bread crumbs, egg yolk, 1 teaspoon salt, and ¼ teaspoon pepper, allspice, and nutmeg. Mix well.

3 Roll meat mixture into sixteen golf ball–sized meatballs and place inside air fryer.

4 Air fry 6 minutes, turning halfway through the cooking time.

5 In a medium skillet over medium-high heat, melt butter and whisk in flour. Continue to mix until butter is fully dissolved and a light beige roux forms, about 6 minutes.

6 Slowly whisk in broth, sour cream, remaining ½ teaspoon salt, and remaining ¼ teaspoon pepper. Continue to cook about 3 minutes, stirring constantly, until sauce is thickened.

7 Pour sauce over cooked meatballs. Serve dish with lingonberry sauce.

PER SERVING (SERVING SIZE: 4 MEATBALLS)

CALORIES: 526 | FAT: 26g | PROTEIN: 23g | SODIUM: 1,441mg | FIBER: 1g | CARBOHYDRATES: 46g | SUGAR: 33g

Cheesy Beef and Rice Casserole

This tasty casserole mixes up quickly, making it a great option for busy weeknights.

Hands-On Time: 20 minutes
Cook Time: 20 minutes
Total Recipe Cost: $10.04

Serves 4

1 pound (93% lean) cooked ground beef
2 cups cooked white rice
2 cups shredded sharp Cheddar cheese, divided
1 (15-ounce) can cream of mushroom soup
½ cup chopped yellow onion
½ cup sour cream
1 tablespoon minced garlic
1 tablespoon Italian seasoning
1 teaspoon salt
1 teaspoon ground black pepper

1 Preheat air fryer to 350°F.

2 In a 7" cake pan, combine ground beef, rice, 1 cup cheese, soup, onion, sour cream, garlic, Italian seasoning, salt, and pepper. Mix well.

3 Place pan inside air fryer. Air fry 15 minutes.

4 Top casserole with remaining 1 cup cheese. Air fry an additional 5 minutes. Serve.

PER SERVING

CALORIES: 651 | FAT: 33g | PROTEIN: 40g | SODIUM: 1,742mg | FIBER: 2g | CARBOHYDRATES: 39g | SUGAR: 2g

Taco Pie

Crescent roll dough is used as the pie crust in this recipe. Some pieces of the dough may need to be torn to fit evenly in the cake pan.

Hands-On Time: 20 minutes
Cook Time: 10 minutes
Total Recipe Cost: $10.71

Serves 4

1 (8-ounce) can refrigerated crescent roll dough
1 pound (93% lean) cooked ground beef
¼ cup taco seasoning
1 cup sour cream
1½ cups crushed tortilla chips
1 cup shredded Mexican cheese blend

PREVENT STICKING

Be sure to grease your pan well prior to cooking the crescent rolls, as they tend to want to stick to the pan.

1 Preheat air fryer to 320°F. Spray a 7" cake pan with olive oil spray and set aside.

2 Unroll crescent roll dough and arrange dough in bottom and on sides of prepared pan.

3 Air fry 6 minutes, then remove pan from air fryer.

4 In a medium bowl, mix ground beef and taco seasoning together. Place mixture on top of cooked dough in pan.

5 Spread sour cream over beef mixture and top with tortilla chips and cheese.

6 Increase temperature on air fryer to 350°F. Air fry 4 minutes until cheese is melted and golden brown. Serve.

PER SERVING

CALORIES: 561 | FAT: 32g | PROTEIN: 16g | SODIUM: 1,232mg | FIBER: 2g | CARBOHYDRATES: 46g | SUGAR: 9g

Beef and Cheese Burritos

Cooking burritos in the air fryer make the tortillas extra crispy and crunchy. This texture takes burritos from ordinary to extraordinary.

Hands-On Time: 15 minutes
Cook Time: 5 minutes
Total Recipe Cost: $5.74

Serves 4

½ pound (93% lean) cooked ground beef
⅛ cup taco seasoning
1 cup refried beans
½ cup red enchilada sauce
4 (10") flour tortillas
1 cup shredded Mexican cheese blend
½ cup sour cream

DON'T HAVE ENCHILADA SAUCE?

You can substitute enchilada sauce with mild salsa or taco sauce. Make sure to taste the sauce before use to ensure it's not too spicy for you or your family.

1 Preheat air fryer to 400°F.

2 In a medium bowl, combine ground beef, taco seasoning, beans, and enchilada sauce. Mix well.

3 Fill the center of each tortilla with beef mixture and top with cheese and sour cream. Roll tortillas into burritos.

4 Spray inside of air fryer with olive oil spray.

5 Place burritos inside air fryer, seam-side down. Spray top of burritos with olive oil spray.

6 Air fry 5 minutes until golden brown. Serve.

PER SERVING

CALORIES: 591 | **FAT:** 23g | **PROTEIN:** 39g | **SODIUM:** 1,494mg | **FIBER:** 6g | **CARBOHYDRATES:** 51g | **SUGAR:** 6g

Lasagna

Lasagna is a classic for a reason. The layers of meat, cheese, and sauce are filling and flavorful. Make sure to wrap the top of your pan in foil for the first part of air frying so the cheese doesn't burn.

Hands-On Time: 20 minutes
Cook Time: 30 minutes
Total Recipe Cost: $7.54

Serves 4

- ½ pound (93% lean) cooked ground beef
- ½ cup ricotta cheese
- 1 tablespoon Italian seasoning
- 1 tablespoon minced garlic
- 1 teaspoon salt
- ½ teaspoon ground black pepper
- ½ (9-ounce) box no-boil lasagna noodles
- 2 cups marinara sauce
- 1 cup shredded mozzarella cheese
- ¼ cup grated Parmesan cheese

1 Preheat air fryer to 320°F. Grease inside of a 7" cake pan and set aside.

2 In a medium bowl, combine ground beef, ricotta, Italian seasoning, garlic, salt, and pepper. Mix until well combined.

3 Layer half of noodles in bottom of prepared pan. Spread 1 cup marinara sauce on top.

4 Pour half of beef mixture over sauce. Top beef mixture with ½ cup mozzarella.

5 Repeat with remaining noodles, sauce, beef mixture, and mozzarella.

6 Sprinkle Parmesan over lasagna and cover pan with foil. Place pan inside air fryer.

7 Air fry 20 minutes, then remove foil. Air fry an additional 10 minutes. Serve warm.

PER SERVING

CALORIES: 394 | FAT: 15g | PROTEIN: 29g | SODIUM: 1,216mg | FIBER: 3g | CARBOHYDRATES: 33g | SUGAR: 5g

Beef Stir-Fry

Making a stir-fry is an incredibly versatile way to use up vegetables that would otherwise not get eaten and end up being wasted. Feel free to substitute the vegetables in this recipe for whatever you have on hand.

Hands-On Time: 15 minutes
Cook Time: 17 minutes
Total Recipe Cost: $10.93

Serves 4

- 1 pound sirloin steak, cut into thin strips
- ¼ cup cornstarch
- ½ teaspoon salt
- ¼ teaspoon ground black pepper
- ⅓ cup orange juice
- ¼ cup low-sodium soy sauce
- 3 tablespoons packed light brown sugar
- 1 tablespoon minced garlic
- 1½ teaspoons sesame oil
- 1 teaspoon ginger paste
- 1 large carrot, peeled and sliced
- 1 cup broccoli florets
- ½ cup sugar snap peas
- 2 tablespoons olive oil

1 In a large bowl, combine steak, cornstarch, salt, and pepper. Toss to evenly coat steak. Discard any excess cornstarch mixture.

2 In a small bowl, whisk together orange juice, soy sauce, brown sugar, garlic, sesame oil, and ginger paste. Pour sauce over steak. Refrigerate 30 minutes.

3 Preheat air fryer to 300°F.

4 Place carrot, broccoli, and snap peas inside air fryer. Drizzle vegetables with olive oil and stir to evenly coat. Air fry 7 minutes. Remove and set aside.

5 Increase temperature on air fryer to 360°F. Remove steak from marinade and place inside air fryer. Air fry 10 minutes.

6 Combine beef and vegetables and serve.

PER SERVING

CALORIES: 333 | FAT: 19g | PROTEIN: 26g | SODIUM: 256mg | FIBER: 2g | CARBOHYDRATES: 9g | SUGAR: 3g

Breaded Pork Chops

Make your own pork chop breading with a combination of panko bread crumbs, Parmesan cheese, and lots of seasonings. Make sure to double-dip them in the eggs and bread crumbs for extra crunch!

Hands-On Time: 20 minutes
Cook Time: 9 minutes
Total Recipe Cost: $7.73

Serves 4

- ¾ cup panko bread crumbs
- ¼ cup grated Parmesan cheese
- 1½ teaspoons salt
- 1¼ teaspoons paprika
- ½ teaspoon garlic powder
- ½ teaspoon onion powder
- ¼ teaspoon chili powder
- ⅛ teaspoon ground black pepper
- 3 large eggs, beaten
- 4 (4-ounce) thick-cut bone-in pork chops

1 Preheat air fryer to 370°F.

2 In a medium shallow bowl, mix together bread crumbs, cheese, salt, paprika, garlic powder, onion powder, chili powder, and pepper. In a second medium shallow bowl, add eggs.

3 Dip pork chops in eggs and shake off any excess, then dip in bread crumb mixture.

4 Dip pork chops once again in eggs and then bread crumb mixture.

5 Spray inside of air fryer with olive oil spray. Arrange pork chops in a single layer inside air fryer. Spray top of pork chops with olive oil spray.

6 Air fry 9 minutes, flipping halfway through the cooking time. Serve.

PER SERVING

CALORIES: 275 | FAT: 8g | PROTEIN: 32g | SODIUM: 1,141mg | FIBER: 0g | CARBOHYDRATES: 17g | SUGAR: 1g

Sausage and Peppers

Sausage and peppers go together like peanut butter and jelly. Use green and red bell peppers for the perfect sweet-savory combination.

Hands-On Time: 15 minutes
Cook Time: 14 minutes
Total Recipe Cost: $5.13

Serves 4

- 1 medium green bell pepper, seeded and sliced
- 1 medium red bell pepper, seeded and sliced
- 1 medium yellow onion, peeled and sliced
- 2 tablespoons olive oil
- 4 (2-ounce) smoked sausages

CHOOSING A SMOKED SAUSAGE

Use your favorite smoked sausage for this recipe. Pork sausages are traditionally used, but they can be substituted with beef or even chicken smoked sausages.

1 Preheat air fryer to 360°F.

2 In a medium bowl, combine peppers, onion, and oil. Toss to evenly coat vegetables with oil.

3 Slice two slits in both side of sausages.

4 Arrange sausages, peppers, and onion inside air fryer.

5 Air fry 14 minutes, stirring halfway through the cooking time. Serve warm.

PER SERVING

CALORIES: 255 | FAT: 20g | PROTEIN: 8g | SODIUM: 483mg | FIBER: 2g | CARBOHYDRATES: 7g | SUGAR: 3g

Mustard-Glazed Pork Tenderloin

Pork tenderloin cooks quickly in the air fryer. The crispy crust on the outside is a perfect complement to the tender pork on the inside.

Hands-On Time: 10 minutes
Cook Time: 20 minutes
Total Recipe Cost: $6.88

Serves 4

1 (1½-pound) pork tenderloin
1 teaspoon Italian seasoning
1 teaspoon salt
½ teaspoon ground black pepper
½ cup packed light brown sugar
3 tablespoons Dijon mustard

COOKING A DIFFERENT-SIZED TENDERLOIN?

This recipe for pork tenderloin was tested using a 1½-pound tenderloin. If using a different weight of meat, the best way to know it is done is by checking the temperature with a meat thermometer. It should be 145°F in the center.

1 Preheat air fryer to 400°F.

2 Pat tenderloin dry. Season with Italian seasoning, salt, and pepper.

3 Place tenderloin inside air fryer.

4 In a small bowl, mix together brown sugar and mustard. Brush mixture over top and sides of tenderloin.

5 Air fry 20 minutes until tenderloin reaches an internal temperature of 145°F. Serve.

PER SERVING

CALORIES: 292 | FAT: 6g | PROTEIN: 30g | SODIUM: 1,182mg | FIBER: 0g | CARBOHYDRATES: 28g | SUGAR: 27g

Garlic-Herb Pork Tenderloin

This simple recipe takes just 10 minutes to prepare and comes out full of flavor. Make sure to fully melt the butter before making the sauce. Otherwise, it won't spread evenly onto the pork tenderloin.

Hands-On Time: 10 minutes
Cook Time: 20 minutes
Total Recipe Cost: $7.59

Serves 4

1 (1½-pound) pork tenderloin
2 tablespoons garlic and herb seasoning
1 teaspoon salt
½ cup unsalted butter, melted

1 Preheat air fryer to 400°F.

2 Pat tenderloin dry. Rub seasoning and salt all over tenderloin.

3 Place tenderloin inside air fryer and brush top and sides with melted butter.

4 Air fry 20 minutes until tenderloin reaches an internal temperature of 145°F. Serve.

PER SERVING

CALORIES: 367 | FAT: 26g | PROTEIN: 30g | SODIUM: 1,437mg | FIBER: 0g | CARBOHYDRATES: 0g | SUGAR: 0g

Italian Meatballs

Italian Meatballs are amazing on pasta and in sub sandwiches. With this recipe, you can have delicious meatballs in very little time! The most time-consuming part of this recipe is rolling the meatballs. They can be made ahead of time and refrigerated up to 24 hours before cooking.

Hands-On Time: 20 minutes
Cook Time: 14 minutes
Total Recipe Cost: $5.93

Serves 4

- 1 pound (93% lean) ground beef
- ¼ cup panko bread crumbs
- ¼ cup whole milk
- 1 tablespoon Worcestershire sauce
- 1¼ teaspoons dried basil, divided
- ½ teaspoon dried parsley
- ½ teaspoon garlic powder
- 1½ teaspoons salt, divided
- ¾ teaspoon ground black pepper, divided
- 1 (15-ounce) can tomato sauce
- 1 (8-ounce) can tomato paste
- ¼ cup water
- ½ teaspoon granulated sugar
- ¼ teaspoon red pepper flakes
- ⅛ teaspoon dried oregano

1. Preheat air fryer to 360°F.

2. In a large bowl, combine ground beef, bread crumbs, milk, Worcestershire sauce, 1 teaspoon basil, parsley, garlic powder, 1 teaspoon salt, and ½ teaspoon black pepper. Mix well.

3. Roll beef mixture into golf ball–sized meatballs. Arrange meatballs inside air fryer.

4. Air fry 4 minutes, turning halfway through the cooking time. Remove meatballs from air fryer and place in a 7" cake pan.

5. In a medium bowl, whisk together tomato sauce, tomato paste, water, sugar, red pepper flakes, oregano, remaining ¼ teaspoon basil, remaining ½ teaspoon salt, and remaining ¼ teaspoon black pepper. Pour sauce over meatballs.

6. Air fry 10 minutes, stirring halfway through the cooking time. Serve.

PER SERVING

CALORIES: 263 | FAT: 7g | PROTEIN: 27g | SODIUM: 1,933mg | FIBER: 4g | CARBOHYDRATES: 24g | SUGAR: 13g

MEATBALL SUBS

To make meatball subs, place cooked meatballs in a hoagie roll and top with provolone cheese. Air fry at 400°F for 2 minutes or until cheese is melted and roll is lightly toasted.

7

Fish and Seafood Main Dishes

Cooking seafood in the air fryer is one of those things you may have never thought of, but it's actually amazing. Air-fried seafood cooks quickly, so it has less time to dry out. Air-fried fish comes out crispy, as if it was deep-fried—without all of the oil. You can make the traditional crispy Fish Sticks and Breaded Scallops in an air fryer, but you can also make Mini Tuna Casseroles, Shrimp Scampi, and Crab Cakes!

Fish Sticks

Fish Sticks are a family favorite! Making them at home is quick and easy, and the air fryer makes them extra crispy! Always choose panko bread crumbs if you can because they make these Fish Sticks extra crispy on the outside. Coating them with a bit of olive oil helps them brown evenly.

Hands-On Time: 15 minutes
Cook Time: 10 minutes
Total Recipe Cost: $6.17

Serves 4

¼ cup cornstarch
1 teaspoon garlic powder
1 teaspoon paprika
1 teaspoon salt
¼ teaspoon ground black pepper
2 large eggs, beaten
1½ cups panko bread crumbs
1 teaspoon Creole seasoning
4 (3-ounce) cod fillets, cut into 1" × 2" strips

1 Preheat air fryer to 400°F.

2 In a medium shallow bowl, whisk together cornstarch, garlic powder, paprika, salt, and pepper. Place eggs in a second medium shallow bowl. In a third medium shallow bowl, mix together bread crumbs and Creole seasoning.

3 Dredge cod in cornstarch mixture. Next, dip in eggs, shaking off any excess. Finally, dip in bread crumb mixture.

4 Spray inside of air fryer with olive oil spray.

5 Arrange cod inside air fryer, spaced ½" apart, and spray with olive oil spray.

6 Air fry 10 minutes, flipping halfway through the cooking time. Fish Sticks are done when they reach an internal temperature of 145°F. Serve warm.

PER SERVING

CALORIES: 228 | FAT: 4g | PROTEIN: 19g | SODIUM: 1,280mg | FIBER: 0g | CARBOHYDRATES: 28g | SUGAR: 1g

Teriyaki Salmon

This delicious dish consists of salmon fillets marinaded in a homemade sauce and air fried to tender perfection.

Hands-On Time: 10 minutes
Cook Time: 8 minutes
Total Recipe Cost: $6.37

Serves 4

- 4 (6-ounce) salmon fillets
- ⅓ cup packed light brown sugar
- 3 tablespoons teriyaki sauce
- 3 tablespoons hoisin sauce
- 3 tablespoons low-sodium soy sauce
- 2 tablespoons minced garlic
- 1 tablespoon white vinegar
- 1 tablespoon sesame oil
- ½ teaspoon ginger paste
- 2 teaspoons sesame seeds

1 Place salmon in a shallow baking dish.

2 In a medium bowl, whisk together brown sugar, teriyaki sauce, hoisin sauce, soy sauce, garlic, vinegar, oil, and ginger paste.

3 Pour sauce over salmon. Refrigerate and let marinate 30 minutes up to 24 hours.

4 Preheat air fryer to 390°F.

5 Remove salmon from marinade and place inside air fryer. Air fry 8 minutes. Salmon is done when it reaches an internal temperature of 145°F.

6 Serve salmon topped with sesame seeds.

PER SERVING

CALORIES: 439 | FAT: 21g | PROTEIN: 36g | SODIUM: 620mg | FIBER: 0g | CARBOHYDRATES: 15g | SUGAR: 12g

Cajun Shrimp "Boil"

Make this Cajun Shrimp "Boil" in your air fryer. It includes all of the fixings: red potatoes, corn on the cob, smoked sausage, and shrimp!

Hands-On Time: 15 minutes
Cook Time: 20 minutes
Total Recipe Cost: $11.54

Serves 4

½ pound baby red potatoes

½ pound andouille sausage

2 medium ears corn, husks removed, halved

1 medium yellow onion, peeled and roughly chopped

2 tablespoons olive oil

3 teaspoons Creole seasoning

12 ounces shrimp, peeled and deveined

1 medium lemon, cut into wedges

1 Preheat air fryer to 400°F.

2 Place potatoes inside air fryer. Air fry 10 minutes until fork-tender.

3 Add sausage, corn, onion, oil, and Creole seasoning to air fryer. Mix well so seasoning is evenly distributed. Air fry 5 minutes.

4 Add shrimp to air fryer and mix. Air fry an additional 5 minutes, stirring halfway through the cooking time. Shrimp boil is done when it reaches an internal temperature of 145°F.

5 Serve with lemon squeezed on top.

PER SERVING

CALORIES: 327 | FAT: 17g | PROTEIN: 23g | SODIUM: 2,204mg | FIBER: 4g | CARBOHYDRATES: 23g | SUGAR: 5g

Salmon Cakes

This recipe calls for fresh cooked salmon, but canned salmon may be used if desired. Making Salmon Cakes is a great way to use up leftover salmon from the Teriyaki Salmon recipe in this chapter.

Hands-On Time: 20 minutes
Cook Time: 7 minutes
Total Recipe Cost: $5.51

Serves 4

½ pound cooked salmon, shredded
2 large eggs, lightly beaten
1 cup panko bread crumbs
2 medium green onions, finely sliced
2 tablespoons chopped fresh flat-leaf parsley
2 tablespoons low-sodium soy sauce
1 tablespoon Worcestershire sauce
1 teaspoon salt
½ teaspoon garlic powder
½ teaspoon cayenne pepper
¼ teaspoon celery seed

1 Preheat air fryer to 370°F.

2 In a large bowl, combine all ingredients and mix well.

3 Form mixture into four equal balls and flatten into 1"-thick patties.

4 Spray inside of air fryer with olive oil spray.

5 Arrange patties inside air fryer in a single layer and spray tops with olive oil spray.

6 Air fry 7 minutes, flipping halfway through the cooking time. Salmon cakes are done when they reach an internal temperature of 145°F. Serve.

PER SERVING

CALORIES: 267 | FAT: 10g | PROTEIN: 19g | SODIUM: 966mg | FIBER: 0g | CARBOHYDRATES: 23g | SUGAR: 2g

Cajun Fish Cakes

Cajun Fish Cakes are a tilapia-based fish cake made with lemon, potato, sour cream, and Cajun seasoning. If you would like to reduce the spiciness, Creole seasoning may be used in place of the Cajun seasoning.

Hands-On Time: 20 minutes
Cook Time: 10 minutes
Total Recipe Cost: $5.01

Serves 4

½ pound cooked tilapia, shredded
1 cup panko bread crumbs
2 large eggs, lightly beaten
½ cup peeled and shredded russet potato
2 tablespoons sour cream
1 tablespoon Cajun seasoning
2 teaspoons lemon juice
¼ teaspoon salt

1 Preheat air fryer to 370°F.

2 In a large bowl, combine all ingredients and mix well.

3 Form mixture into four equal balls and flatten into 1"-thick patties.

4 Spray inside of air fryer with olive oil spray.

5 Arrange patties inside air fryer in a single layer and spray tops with olive oil spray.

6 Air fry 10 minutes, flipping halfway through the cooking time. Fish cakes are done when they reach an internal temperature of 145°F. Serve.

PER SERVING

CALORIES: 235 | FAT: 6g | PROTEIN: 22g | SODIUM: 451mg | FIBER: 0g | CARBOHYDRATES: 24g | SUGAR: 1g

Crab Cakes

Enjoy these delicious Crab Cakes as a meal or appetizer at home. Using canned crabmeat makes this recipe affordable enough for an ordinary Saturday night.

Hands-On Time: 20 minutes
Cook Time: 10 minutes
Total Recipe Cost: $6.63

Serves 4

2 (6-ounce) cans crabmeat, drained
¾ cup panko bread crumbs
⅓ cup mayonnaise
1 large egg, lightly beaten
2 tablespoons chopped fresh Italian flat-leaf parsley
2 tablespoons Dijon mustard
2 teaspoons Worcestershire sauce
1 teaspoon Creole seasoning
½ teaspoon salt
¼ teaspoon ground black pepper

1 Preheat air fryer to 370°F.

2 In a large bowl, combine all ingredients and mix well.

3 Form mixture into four equal balls and flatten into 1"-thick patties.

4 Spray inside of air fryer with olive oil spray.

5 Arrange patties inside air fryer in a single layer and spray tops with olive oil spray.

6 Air fry 10 minutes, flipping halfway through the cooking time. Crab Cakes are done when they reach an internal temperature of 165°F. Serve.

PER SERVING

CALORIES: 284 | FAT: 16g | PROTEIN: 15g | SODIUM: 1,370mg | FIBER: 0g | CARBOHYDRATES: 16g | SUGAR: 1g

Bang Bang Shrimp

Bang Bang Shrimp features crispy shrimp topped with a creamy, spicy sauce. Make sure to plan ahead for soaking the shrimp in buttermilk, as it makes a big difference in tenderizing the shrimp before cooking.

Hands-On Time: 15 minutes
Cook Time: 5 minutes
Total Recipe Cost: $6.62

Serves 4

12 ounces shrimp, peeled and deveined
1 cup buttermilk
¼ cup cornstarch
½ cup mayonnaise
¼ cup Thai sweet chili sauce
¼ teaspoon sriracha

1 Place shrimp in a shallow baking dish and cover with buttermilk. Refrigerate 20 minutes.

2 Preheat air fryer to 400°F.

3 Remove shrimp from buttermilk and dip in cornstarch, shaking off any excess.

4 Spray both sides of shrimp with olive oil spray and place inside air fryer in an even layer.

5 Air fry 5 minutes, flipping halfway through the cooking time. Shrimp is done when it reaches an internal temperature of 145°F.

6 In a small bowl, whisk together mayonnaise, chili sauce, and sriracha.

7 Top shrimp with sauce. Serve.

PER SERVING

CALORIES: 305 | FAT: 21g | PROTEIN: 12g | SODIUM: 913mg | FIBER: 0g | CARBOHYDRATES: 14g | SUGAR: 10g

Fish Tacos

These classic Fish Tacos are made with air-fried cod fillets and topped with a homemade creamy taco sauce and red cabbage—it doesn't get much yummier than this!

Hands-On Time: 20 minutes
Cook Time: 7 minutes
Total Recipe Cost: $11.31

Serves 4

¼ cup taco seasoning
3 tablespoons olive oil
1 pound cod fillets
3 tablespoons mayonnaise
3 tablespoons sour cream
1 tablespoon lime juice
1 teaspoon sriracha
⅛ teaspoon garlic powder
⅛ teaspoon ground cumin
8 (6") corn tortillas
1 cup shredded red cabbage

1 Preheat air fryer to 400°F.

2 In a small bowl, whisk together taco seasoning and oil. Brush mixture over cod.

3 Place cod inside air fryer. Air fry 7 minutes.

4 Meanwhile, in a small bowl, whisk together mayonnaise, sour cream, lime juice, sriracha, garlic powder, and cumin.

5 Serve cod in tortillas, topped with sauce and cabbage.

PER SERVING (SERVING SIZE: 2 TACOS)

CALORIES: 394 | FAT: 21g | PROTEIN: 21g | SODIUM: 1,079mg | FIBER: 5g | CARBOHYDRATES: 29g | SUGAR: 3g

MAKING IT SPICY

If you want a spicier sauce for your Fish Tacos, add 1 teaspoon of adobo sauce from a can of chipotle peppers in adobo sauce. It adds a great flavor, but a little goes a long way for spiciness.

Panko-Crusted Tilapia

Breaded tilapia is a must-try for any air fryer cook. Be sure to spray the outside with a light coating of oil to help the breading brown evenly. Panko bread crumbs (Japanese bread crumbs) add a better crunch than traditional bread crumbs, so use them if you can.

Hands-On Time: 20 minutes
Cook Time: 7 minutes
Total Recipe Cost: $6.90

Serves 4

4 (6-ounce) tilapia fillets
2 teaspoons salt, divided
1 teaspoon ground black pepper, divided
1 teaspoon garlic powder, divided
1½ cups panko bread crumbs
½ teaspoon paprika
½ teaspoon dried parsley
½ cup cornstarch
4 large eggs, beaten

1 Preheat air fryer to 370°F.

2 Pat tilapia dry and rub 1 teaspoon salt, ½ teaspoon pepper, and ½ teaspoon garlic powder on both sides of the fish.

3 In a medium shallow bowl, mix together bread crumbs, remaining 1 teaspoon salt, remaining ½ teaspoon pepper, remaining ½ teaspoon garlic powder, paprika, and parsley.

4 Place cornstarch in a separate medium shallow bowl, and place eggs in a third medium shallow bowl.

5 Dredge tilapia in cornstarch. Then dip in eggs, shaking to remove any excess, and finally in bread crumb mixture.

6 Dip coated tilapia a second time in eggs and then again in bread crumb mixture.

7 Spray inside of air fryer with olive oil spray.

8 Place tilapia inside air fryer in a single layer and spray with olive oil spray.

9 Air fry 7 minutes. Tilapia is done when it reaches an internal temperature of 145°F. Serve.

PER SERVING

CALORIES: 331 | FAT: 6g | PROTEIN: 40g | SODIUM: 1,051mg | FIBER: 0g | CARBOHYDRATES: 28g | SUGAR: 1g

Shrimp Scampi

These tender shrimp cooked in a buttery sauce can be enjoyed on their own or over angel hair pasta. This dish also makes great leftovers. Double the batch and enjoy it the next day for lunch too.

Hands-On Time: 20 minutes
Cook Time: 7 minutes
Total Recipe Cost: $6.63

Serves 4

¼ cup minced garlic
¼ cup unsalted butter, melted
2 tablespoons chicken broth
1 tablespoon lemon juice
1 teaspoon salt
1 teaspoon red pepper flakes
½ teaspoon ground black pepper
12 ounces shrimp, peeled and deveined

1 Place a 7" cake pan inside air fryer. Preheat air fryer to 400°F.

2 In a medium bowl, whisk together garlic, melted butter, broth, lemon juice, salt, red pepper flakes, and black pepper.

3 Place shrimp inside pan. Pour sauce over shrimp.

4 Air fry 7 minutes, stirring halfway through the cooking time. Shrimp is done when it reaches an internal temperature of 145°F. Serve.

PER SERVING

CALORIES: 175 | FAT: 11g | PROTEIN: 12g | SODIUM: 1,094mg | FIBER: 0g | CARBOHYDRATES: 4g | SUGAR: 0g

Chili Lime Tilapia

The yummy combination of chili and lime enhances the flavor of the tilapia. With just four ingredients, this recipe is perfect for a quick and affordable weeknight meal.

Hands-On Time: 10 minutes
Cook Time: 7 minutes
Total Recipe Cost: $5.01

Serves 4

4 tablespoons lime juice
3 tablespoons chili powder
½ teaspoon salt
4 (6-ounce) tilapia fillets

1 Preheat air fryer to 400°F.

2 In a small bowl, whisk together lime juice, chili powder, and salt.

3 Brush sauce onto both sides of tilapia.

4 Arrange tilapia inside air fryer in a single layer.

5 Air fry 7 minutes. Tilapia is done when it reaches an internal temperature of 145°F. Serve.

PER SERVING

CALORIES: 183 | FAT: 3g | PROTEIN: 35g | SODIUM: 551mg | FIBER: 2g | CARBOHYDRATES: 4g | SUGAR: 1g

Honey Garlic Salmon

Serve this with a simple steamed vegetable like carrots.

Hands-On Time: 10 minutes
Cook Time: 8 minutes
Total Recipe Cost: $6.61

Serves 4

4 (6-ounce) salmon fillets
1 teaspoon salt
½ teaspoon ground black pepper
½ cup honey
4 tablespoons low-sodium soy sauce
2 tablespoons minced garlic
2 tablespoons rice wine vinegar
1 teaspoon sesame oil
2 teaspoons sesame seeds

1 Preheat air fryer to 390°F.

2 Season salmon with salt and pepper. Place inside air fryer in an even layer. Air fry 8 minutes. Salmon is done when it reaches an internal temperature of 145°F.

3 In a small bowl, whisk together honey, soy sauce, garlic, vinegar, and oil.

4 Pour sauce over salmon and top with sesame seeds. Serve.

PER SERVING

CALORIES: 522 | FAT: 20g | PROTEIN: 37g | SODIUM: 1,117mg | FIBER: 0g | CARBOHYDRATES: 39g | SUGAR: 36g

Fried Catfish

Catfish marinated in buttermilk and then dredged in cornmeal makes for perfectly crispy Fried Catfish. Frozen is the most affordable way to buy catfish. If you can't find frozen catfish, ask the person in the seafood department if they have any fresh catfish on hand.

Hands-On Time: 10 minutes
Cook Time: 15 minutes
Total Recipe Cost: $8.99

Serves 4

4 (6-ounce) catfish fillets
1 cup buttermilk
1½ cups cornmeal
½ cup all-purpose flour
1 teaspoon Old Bay Seasoning
1 teaspoon salt
½ teaspoon ground black pepper

PREPARING AHEAD OF TIME

If you want to prep this recipe early, the catfish can be soaked in buttermilk for up to 2 hours in the refrigerator.

1 Place catfish in a shallow baking dish and cover in buttermilk. Soak catfish 20 minutes in refrigerator.

2 Preheat air fryer to 400°F.

3 In a medium bowl, whisk together cornmeal, flour, Old Bay Seasoning, salt, and pepper.

4 Remove catfish from buttermilk and dredge in cornmeal mixture, ensuring catfish is evenly coated on both sides.

5 Spray inside of air fryer with olive oil spray.

6 Place catfish in a single layer inside air fryer and spray tops with olive oil spray.

7 Air fry 10 minutes, flip catfish, and then air fry 5 more minutes. Catfish is done when it reaches an internal temperature of 145°F. Serve.

PER SERVING

CALORIES: 317 | FAT: 9g | PROTEIN: 29g | SODIUM: 541mg | FIBER: 2g | CARBOHYDRATES: 24g | SUGAR: 0g

Maple-Glazed Salmon

This dish consists of salmon fillets seasoned to perfection and topped with a sweet and spicy sauce. Omit the salt if you're using full-sodium soy sauce.

Hands-On Time: 15 minutes
Cook Time: 8 minutes
Total Recipe Cost: $6.97

Serves 4

- ½ teaspoon salt
- ½ teaspoon garlic powder
- ½ teaspoon onion powder
- ¼ teaspoon paprika
- ¼ teaspoon ground black pepper
- ¼ teaspoon Creole seasoning
- ⅛ teaspoon cayenne pepper
- 4 (6-ounce) salmon fillets
- ½ cup pure maple syrup
- 1 tablespoon packed light brown sugar
- 1 tablespoon low-sodium soy sauce
- 2 teaspoons minced garlic
- 1 teaspoon red pepper flakes

1 Line bottom of air fryer with foil and fold up sides to create a bowl. Preheat air fryer to 390°F.

2 In a small bowl, mix together salt, garlic powder, onion powder, paprika, black pepper, Creole seasoning, and cayenne pepper. Rub seasoning all over salmon.

3 Place salmon in foil bowl.

4 In a second small bowl, whisk together maple syrup, brown sugar, soy sauce, garlic, and red pepper flakes. Pour sauce over salmon.

5 Air fry 8 minutes. Serve.

PER SERVING

CALORIES: 476 | FAT: 18g | PROTEIN: 35g | SODIUM: 504mg |
FIBER: 0g | CARBOHYDRATES: 31g | SUGAR: 27g

Mini Tuna Casseroles

This recipe is a tuna casserole in muffin form! These bite-sized casseroles are a combination of tuna, shell-shaped pasta, cheese, and peas and could not be more delicious!

Hands-On Time: 20 minutes
Cook Time: 14 minutes
Total Recipe Cost: $5.80

Serves 6

2 (5-ounce) cans tuna, drained and flaked
1 (10.5-ounce) can cream of mushroom soup
½ pound small shell-shaped pasta, cooked according to package directions
1 cup shredded sharp Cheddar cheese, divided
¾ cup frozen peas, thawed
1 teaspoon salt, divided
½ teaspoon garlic powder
½ teaspoon ground black pepper
½ cup panko bread crumbs
2 tablespoons unsalted butter, melted

1 Preheat air fryer to 350°F. Grease a six-hole silicone egg mold and set aside.

2 In a large bowl, combine tuna, soup, cooked pasta, ½ cup cheese, peas, ¾ teaspoon salt, garlic powder, and pepper. Mix well.

3 Scoop tuna mixture into prepared egg mold. Place egg mold inside air fryer. Air fry 10 minutes.

4 In a small bowl, mix together bread crumbs, melted butter, and remaining ¼ teaspoon salt.

5 Sprinkle bread crumb mixture over each Mini Tuna Casserole. Top with remaining ½ cup cheese.

6 Air fry an additional 4 minutes until golden brown on top. Serve warm.

PER SERVING

CALORIES: 360 | **FAT:** 13g | **PROTEIN:** 16g | **SODIUM:** 935mg | **FIBER:** 3g | **CARBOHYDRATES:** 41g | **SUGAR:** 2g

Spicy Shrimp

This recipe features shrimp coated in a delectable combination of spices and topped with butter and lemon juice. The spice can be increased or decreased by adjusting the cayenne pepper in this recipe.

Hands-On Time: 10 minutes
Cook Time: 5 minutes
Total Recipe Cost: $5.96

Serves 4

2 tablespoons lemon juice
12 ounces raw shrimp, peeled and deveined
2 tablespoons unsalted butter, melted
1 teaspoon salt
½ teaspoon garlic powder
½ teaspoon onion powder
½ teaspoon ground black pepper
½ teaspoon chili powder
½ teaspoon granulated sugar
¼ teaspoon cayenne pepper

1. Preheat air fryer to 400°F.

2. Brush lemon juice on both sides of shrimp and then top with melted butter.

3. In a small bowl, mix together salt, garlic powder, onion powder, black pepper, chili powder, sugar, and cayenne pepper. Sprinkle seasoning on both sides of shrimp.

4. Place shrimp inside air fryer in an even layer.

5. Air fry 5 minutes, shaking halfway through the cooking time. Shrimp is done when it reaches an internal temperature of 145°F. Serve.

PER SERVING

CALORIES: 118 | FAT: 6g | PROTEIN: 12g | SODIUM: 1,072mg | FIBER: 0g | CARBOHYDRATES: 3g | SUGAR: 1g

Lemon Garlic Tilapia

Tilapia cooked in a sauce of melted butter, lemon, and garlic and topped with red pepper flakes—simple yet delicious! As with the Maple-Glazed Salmon and Parmesan Tilapia recipes in this chapter, the foil bowl is important to keep the sauce on the fish. If you don't have foil on hand, a 7" cake pan may be used instead.

Hands-On Time: 10 minutes
Cook Time: 7 minutes
Total Recipe Cost: $5.14

Serves 4

¼ cup unsalted butter, melted
2 tablespoons lemon juice
1 tablespoon lemon zest
2 tablespoons minced garlic
1 teaspoon salt
1 teaspoon red pepper flakes
¼ teaspoon ground black pepper
4 (6-ounce) tilapia fillets

1 Line bottom of air fryer with foil and fold up sides to create a bowl. Preheat air fryer to 370°F.

2 In a medium bowl, mix together melted butter, lemon juice, lemon zest, garlic, salt, red pepper flakes, and black pepper.

3 Place tilapia in foil bowl and top with butter mixture.

4 Air fry 7 minutes. Serve.

PER SERVING

CALORIES: 273 | FAT: 13g | PROTEIN: 35g | SODIUM: 671mg | FIBER: 0g | CARBOHYDRATES: 2g | SUGAR: 0g

Parmesan Tilapia

This dish features fresh tilapia topped with a buttery Parmesan sauce. Don't skip the step for creating a foil bowl, or the sauce will fall off of the fish.

Hands-On Time: 15 minutes
Cook Time: 7 minutes
Total Recipe Cost: $6.89

Serves 4

- ½ cup grated Parmesan cheese
- ¼ cup unsalted butter, melted
- 3 tablespoons mayonnaise
- 2 tablespoons lemon juice
- ½ teaspoon dried dill weed
- 1 teaspoon salt
- ½ teaspoon ground black pepper
- 4 (6-ounce) tilapia fillets

1 Line bottom of air fryer with foil and fold up sides to create a bowl. Preheat air fryer to 370°F.

2 In a medium bowl, mix together cheese, melted butter, mayonnaise, lemon juice, dill, salt, and pepper.

3 Place tilapia in foil bowl and top with cheese mixture.

4 Air fry 7 minutes. Tilapia is done when it reaches an internal temperature of 145°F. Serve.

PER SERVING

CALORIES: 389 | FAT: 24g | PROTEIN: 38g | SODIUM: 962mg | FIBER: 0g | CARBOHYDRATES: 3g | SUGAR: 0g

Tilapia and Squash Casserole

Fish casseroles are a nice change of pace from traditional fish recipes. This dish is a feast for the eyes and the stomach with its bright and colorful combination of tilapia, yellow summer squash, and green zucchini.

Hands-On Time: 15 minutes
Cook Time: 9 minutes
Total Recipe Cost: $4.37

Serves 4

- ½ pound tilapia, cut into 2" chunks
- 1 medium summer squash, sliced and halved
- 1 medium zucchini, sliced and halved
- ¼ cup grated Parmesan cheese
- 2 tablespoons olive oil
- 1 tablespoon lemon pepper seasoning
- 1 teaspoon salt
- 1 teaspoon red pepper flakes
- ½ teaspoon garlic powder
- ½ teaspoon ground black pepper

1 Preheat air fryer to 350°F.

2 In a 7" cake pan, combine all ingredients and mix well.

3 Place pan inside air fryer and air fry 9 minutes, stirring every 3 minutes. Casserole is done when tilapia reaches an internal temperature of 145°F. Serve.

PER SERVING

CALORIES: 157 | FAT: 9g | PROTEIN: 14g | SODIUM: 817mg | FIBER: 1g | CARBOHYDRATES: 5g | SUGAR: 2g

Garlic Parmesan Shrimp

Soaking the shrimp in buttermilk helps to tenderize it. Then it's coated in a combination of panko bread crumbs and grated Parmesan cheese for a flavorful crunch you'll be sure to love.

Hands-On Time: 10 minutes
Cook Time: 5 minutes
Total Recipe Cost: $8.71

Serves 4

12 ounces shrimp, peeled and deveined
1 cup buttermilk
½ cup panko bread crumbs
½ cup grated Parmesan cheese
2 tablespoons garlic powder
1 teaspoon paprika
1 teaspoon salt
½ teaspoon ground black pepper
¼ cup cornstarch
2 large eggs, beaten

1   Place shrimp in a shallow baking dish and cover with buttermilk. Let soak in refrigerator 20 minutes.

2   Preheat air fryer to 400°F.

3   In a medium shallow bowl, mix together bread crumbs, cheese, garlic powder, paprika, salt, and pepper.

4   Place cornstarch in a second medium shallow bowl, and place eggs in a third medium shallow bowl.

5   Remove shrimp from buttermilk and dredge in cornstarch. Next, dip shrimp in eggs and shake off any excess. Finally, dip shrimp in bread crumb mixture.

6   Dip coated shrimp a second time in eggs and then again in bread crumb mixture.

7   Spray both sides of shrimp with olive oil spray. Arrange shrimp in an even layer inside air fryer.

8   Air fry 5 minutes, flipping halfway through the cooking time. Serve warm.

PER SERVING

CALORIES: 217 | FAT: 5g | PROTEIN: 19g | SODIUM: 1,342mg | FIBER: 1g | CARBOHYDRATES: 21g | SUGAR: 1g

Breaded Scallops

In this recipe you'll discover sea scallops seasoned to perfection and coated in panko bread crumbs for an easy but satisfying meal. Sea scallops can be on the more expensive side. It's best to purchase them when they are on sale in the seafood department.

Hands-On Time: 25 minutes
Cook Time: 6 minutes
Total Recipe Cost: $6.02

Serves 4

1 cup panko bread crumbs
1 teaspoon salt
1 teaspoon paprika
½ teaspoon garlic powder
½ teaspoon ground black
    pepper
¼ cup cornstarch
2 large eggs, beaten
12 ounces sea scallops

1 Preheat air fryer to 400°F.

2 In a medium shallow bowl, mix together bread crumbs, salt, paprika, garlic powder, and pepper.

3 Place cornstarch in a second medium shallow bowl, and eggs in a third medium shallow bowl.

4 Dredge scallops in cornstarch. Then dip in eggs, shaking off any excess. Finally, dip in bread crumb mixture.

5 Dip coated scallops a second time in eggs and then again in bread crumb mixture.

6 Spray both sides of scallops with olive oil spray. Arrange scallops inside air fryer in an even layer.

7 Air fry 6 minutes, flipping halfway through the cooking time. Serve warm.

PER SERVING

CALORIES: 212 | FAT: 4g | PROTEIN: 17g | SODIUM: 1,005mg | FIBER: 0g | CARBOHYDRATES: 27g | SUGAR: 1g

Beer-Battered Cod

Beer-Battered Cod can be a bit tricky. Start by coating the fish in beer batter, followed by a dry batter. Finally, coat the whole thing in olive oil spray.

Hands-On Time: 25 minutes
Cook Time: 7 minutes
Total Recipe Cost: $7.84

Serves 4

1 cup beer
1¾ cups all-purpose flour, divided
1 large egg
1½ teaspoons salt, divided
1 teaspoon baking soda
½ teaspoon ground black pepper, divided
1 tablespoon paprika
1 teaspoon Old Bay Seasoning
4 (6-ounce) cod steaks

1 Preheat air fryer to 370°F.

2 In a medium shallow bowl, mix together beer, 1 cup flour, egg, 1 teaspoon salt, baking soda, and ¼ teaspoon pepper.

3 In a separate medium shallow bowl, whisk together remaining ¾ cup flour, paprika, Old Bay Seasoning, remaining ½ teaspoon salt, and remaining ¼ teaspoon pepper.

4 Dip cod in beer mixture and then in flour mixture.

5 Spray inside of air fryer with olive oil spray. Coat well to prevent sticking. Spray all sides of cod with olive oil spray.

6 Air fry 7 minutes, flipping halfway through the cooking time. Cod is done when it reaches an internal temperature of 145°F. Serve.

PER SERVING

CALORIES: 317 | FAT: 2g | PROTEIN: 33g | SODIUM: 1,571mg | FIBER: 2g | CARBOHYDRATES: 37g | SUGAR: 0g

8

Vegetarian Main Dishes

You don't have to be a vegetarian to go meatless. Vegetarian main dishes are all about swapping meat for hearty vegetables, potatoes, and/or beans. Vegetarian dishes are also a great way to save money, as meat tends to be the most expensive part of many meals. In this chapter, you will learn how to make Vegetable Garden Pizzas, Corn Fritters, Fried Ravioli, Portobello Mushroom Burgers, and so much more!

Broccoli and Cheese–Loaded Baked Potatoes

The combination of broccoli, cheese, and potato is absolutely heavenly. The potatoes may be air fried ahead of time and stored in the refrigerator for up to 4 days, until you are ready to complete the recipe.

Hands-On Time: 20 minutes
Cook Time: 1 hour, 6 minutes
Total Recipe Cost: $5.56

Serves 4

- 4 large russet potatoes
- 2 cups chopped broccoli florets
- 2 tablespoons olive oil
- 1½ teaspoons salt, divided
- ½ teaspoon ground black pepper
- ½ teaspoon garlic powder
- 4 teaspoons unsalted butter
- ½ cup shredded sharp Cheddar cheese

FROZEN BROCCOLI?

Cooking with frozen vegetables is a great way to save money! If you're using frozen broccoli florets, let them defrost at room temperature for an hour before cooking and drain any excess water.

1. Preheat air fryer to 400°F.

2. Poke potatoes all over with the tines of a fork. Place potatoes inside air fryer and air fry 45 minutes.

3. Flip potatoes over and air fry an additional 10 minutes. Remove potatoes from air fryer and set aside.

4. Reduce heat on air fryer to 300°F.

5. In a large bowl, combine broccoli, oil, 1 teaspoon salt, pepper, and garlic powder. Toss to coat.

6. Place broccoli inside air fryer and air fry 8 minutes, shaking or turning halfway through the cooking time.

7. Slice top of each potato open lengthwise.

8. Spread 1 teaspoon butter inside each potato and sprinkle with remaining ½ teaspoon salt.

9. Gently pull potatoes apart and place cooked broccoli inside each and top with cheese.

10. Increase temperature on air fryer to 400°F.

11. Carefully place loaded potatoes inside air fryer. Air fry 3 minutes until cheese is melted. Serve.

PER SERVING

CALORIES: 457 | FAT: 15g | PROTEIN: 13g | SODIUM: 1,020mg | FIBER: 8g | CARBOHYDRATES: 68g | SUGAR: 4g

Parmesan Garlic Spaghetti Squash

This delicious take on pasta is made with spaghetti squash that is air fried to perfection and tossed with fresh garlic and Parmesan cheese. You may need to work in batches to prepare this recipe. Simply wrap the cooked spaghetti squash in foil and set in a warm place until the remaining squash has finished cooking.

Hands-On Time: 20 minutes
Cook Time: 20 minutes (per batch)
Total Recipe Cost: $8.53

Serves 4

1 (4-pound) spaghetti squash
4 teaspoons olive oil
1 cup grated Parmesan cheese
1 tablespoon minced garlic
2 teaspoons garlic powder
1½ teaspoons salt
½ teaspoon ground black pepper
½ teaspoon dried parsley

CHOOSING A SPAGHETTI SQUASH

When shopping for spaghetti squash, look for ones free of bruises and blemishes. It is also best to look for squash that are very yellow, as that indicates ripeness. A small spaghetti squash is roughly 4 pounds, but weighing it helps with accuracy. If you are using a larger spaghetti squash, 5 minutes of air fry time may need to be added.

1   Preheat air fryer to 360°F.

2   Slice ¼" off ends of each squash.

3   Cut each squash in half lengthwise, trying to cut as evenly as possible. Use a spoon to scoop out seeds of squash.

4   Drizzle inside of each half with oil.

5   Place squash inside air fryer, cut-side up. Air fry 20 minutes until fork-tender (you may need to work in batches).

6   Remove squash from air fryer and use a fork to fluff up squash and then scoop the insides into a large bowl.

7   Mix in cheese, minced garlic, garlic powder, salt, pepper, and parsley. Serve.

PER SERVING

CALORIES: 205 | **FAT:** 11g | **PROTEIN:** 9g | **SODIUM:** 1,359mg | **FIBER:** 3g | **CARBOHYDRATES:** 18g | **SUGAR:** 5g

Spaghetti Squash Tacos

Enjoy this spin on vegetarian tacos. They are filled with black beans, cheese, tomatoes, avocado, salsa, and flavorfully air-fried spaghetti squash.

Hands-On Time: 20 minutes
Cook Time: 20 minutes
Total Recipe Cost: $11.87

Serves 4

1 (2-pound) spaghetti squash
2 teaspoons olive oil
1 teaspoon salt
2 teaspoons chili powder
2 teaspoons ground cumin
½ teaspoon cayenne pepper
8 (6") corn tortillas, warmed
1 (16-ounce) can black beans, drained and rinsed
1 cup diced tomatoes
1 medium avocado, peeled, pitted, and chopped
½ cup medium salsa
½ cup crumbled cotija cheese

1 Preheat air fryer to 360°F.

2 Slice ¼" off end of each side of squash.

3 Cut squash in half lengthwise, trying to cut as evenly as possible. Use a spoon to scoop out seeds of squash.

4 Drizzle inside of each half with oil.

5 Place squash inside air fryer, cut-side up. Air fry 20 minutes until fork-tender.

6 Remove squash from air fryer and use a fork to fluff up squash and then scoop the insides into a large bowl.

7 Add salt, chili powder, cumin, and cayenne pepper and mix well.

8 Scoop squash into tortillas and top with beans, tomato, avocado, salsa, and cheese. Serve.

PER SERVING (SERVING SIZE: 2 TACOS)

CALORIES: 374 | FAT: 13g | PROTEIN: 14g | SODIUM: 1,404mg | FIBER: 15g | CARBOHYDRATES: 51g | SUGAR: 5g

Buttermilk Fried Mushrooms

This vegetarian take on fried chicken uses oyster mushrooms. They hold on well to the panko coating and come out extra crispy in the air fryer.

Hands-On Time: 20 minutes
Cook Time: 8 minutes
Total Recipe Cost: $10.11

Serves 4

12 ounces oyster mushrooms
3 cups buttermilk
1 cup cornstarch
4 large eggs, beaten
2 cups panko bread crumbs
1½ teaspoons salt
1½ teaspoons garlic powder
1½ teaspoons paprika
½ teaspoon ground black pepper

1 Place mushrooms in a shallow baking dish and pour buttermilk over mushrooms and let marinate 20 minutes at room temperature.

2 Preheat air fryer to 370°F.

3 Place cornstarch in a medium shallow bowl. Place eggs in a second medium shallow bowl. In a third medium shallow bowl, combine bread crumbs, salt, garlic powder, paprika, and pepper.

4 Drain buttermilk from mushrooms.

5 Dredge mushrooms in cornstarch, turning to coat. Next, dip mushrooms in eggs, shaking off any excess. Finally, dip mushrooms in bread crumb mixture, ensuring all sides are coated.

6 Arrange mushrooms in a single layer inside air fryer and coat well with olive oil spray.

7 Air fry 8 minutes. Serve.

PER SERVING

CALORIES: 290 | FAT: 4g | PROTEIN: 11g | SODIUM: 735mg |
FIBER: 2g | CARBOHYDRATES: 52g | SUGAR: 4g

Italian Portobello Mushroom Steaks

Make your own vegetarian "steaks" with this delicious recipe. Portobello mushrooms absorb whatever flavors you add to them. In this recipe, they're soaked in red wine vinegar, olive oil, and Italian seasoning before they're air fried.

Hands-On Time: 15 minutes
Cook Time: 8 minutes
Total Recipe Cost: $7.11

Serves 4

- 4 large portobello mushrooms, stems removed
- ½ cup red wine vinegar
- ½ cup extra-virgin olive oil
- 1 teaspoon salt
- 1 teaspoon Italian seasoning

CLEANING PORTOBELLO MUSHROOMS

It's important not to rinse portobello mushrooms, as they will absorb all of the water and not absorb the marinade! Instead, use a damp paper towel to wipe them well before marinating.

1 Preheat air fryer to 400°F. Arrange mushrooms in a single layer in a shallow baking dish, top-side down.

2 In a small bowl, whisk together vinegar, oil, salt, and Italian seasoning. Pour mixture over mushrooms and let marinate 20 minutes at room temperature.

3 Spray inside of air fryer with olive oil spray.

4 Place marinated mushrooms inside air fryer in a single layer.

5 Air fry 8 minutes. Serve.

PER SERVING

CALORIES: 115 | FAT: 11g | PROTEIN: 2g | SODIUM: 240mg | FIBER: 1g | CARBOHYDRATES: 3g | SUGAR: 2g

Cheddar Apple Grilled Cheese Sandwiches

Grilled cheese sandwiches in the air fryer come out extra crispy with perfectly melted cheese. Make sure to secure the two slices of bread well with toothpicks. Otherwise, your bread and filling may fly around inside the air fryer.

Hands-On Time: 12 minutes
Cook Time: 8 minutes (per batch)
Total Recipe Cost: $4.30

Serves 4

- 4 teaspoons salted butter
- 8 (¾"-thick) slices sourdough bread
- 8 (1-ounce) slices sharp Cheddar cheese
- 1 medium Granny Smith apple, cored and thinly sliced

WANT A CLASSIC GRILLED CHEESE?

If you are looking for a classic grilled cheese sandwich, simply omit the apple and add an extra slice of cheese. Use your favorite cheese and cook as directed in the recipe.

1 Preheat air fryer to 400°F.

2 Spread butter on one side of each bread slice.

3 Build each sandwich with 2 bread slices (butter-side out) and 2 cheese slices. Evenly place 2 apple slices in center of each sandwich.

4 Hold sandwiches together with toothpicks and place inside air fryer (you may need to work in batches).

5 Air fry 8 minutes, flipping halfway through the cooking time. Serve.

PER SERVING

CALORIES: 438 | FAT: 22g | PROTEIN: 19g | SODIUM: 643mg | FIBER: 3g | CARBOHYDRATES: 34g | SUGAR: 7g

Bean and Rice–Stuffed Bell Peppers

Stuffed bell peppers are extremely frugal and filling. This recipe substitutes ground beef with the less expensive black beans. If you prefer pinto beans, you can use them in place of the black beans.

Hands-On Time: 15 minutes
Cook Time: 15 minutes
Total Recipe Cost: $6.02

Serves 4

- 1 (15.5-ounce) can black beans, drained and rinsed
- ½ (15-ounce) can whole kernel corn, drained
- ½ cup cooked white rice
- 1 (4-ounce) can diced mild green chilies
- 1 cup shredded Mexican cheese blend, divided
- ¾ teaspoon salt
- ½ teaspoon onion powder
- ¼ teaspoon ground cumin
- ½ teaspoon dried oregano
- ¼ teaspoon cayenne pepper
- ¼ teaspoon ground black pepper
- 4 large red bell peppers, tops sliced off and seeds removed

1. Preheat air fryer to 350°F.

2. In a medium bowl, combine beans, corn, rice, chilies, ¾ cup cheese, salt, onion powder, cumin, oregano, cayenne pepper, and black pepper. Mix well.

3. Stuff each bell pepper with bean mixture. Carefully place bell peppers inside air fryer. Air fry 12 minutes.

4. Top bell peppers with remaining ¼ cup cheese.

5. Air fry an additional 3 minutes. Serve.

PER SERVING

CALORIES: 311 | FAT: 8g | PROTEIN: 16g | SODIUM: 935mg | FIBER: 13g | CARBOHYDRATES: 42g | SUGAR: 9g

Stuffed Pepper Casserole

This recipe makes classic stuffed peppers in a casserole form! This cheesy casserole is packed full of black beans, green chilies, corn, and rice. The casserole can be prepared up to 24 hours in advance and stored in the refrigerator until ready to be air fried.

Hands-On Time: 15 minutes
Cook Time: 20 minutes
Total Recipe Cost: $5.46

Serves 4

1 (15.5-ounce) can black beans, drained and rinsed
1 (4-ounce) can diced mild green chilies
½ (15-ounce) can whole kernel corn, drained
1¼ cups shredded Mexican cheese blend, divided
1 cup cooked rice
1 small yellow bell pepper, seeded and diced
1 small orange bell pepper, seeded and diced
¾ teaspoon salt
½ teaspoon onion powder
¼ teaspoon ground cumin
½ teaspoon dried oregano
¼ teaspoon cayenne pepper
¼ teaspoon ground black pepper

1 Preheat air fryer to 320°F. Grease a 7" cake pan and set aside.

2 In a medium bowl, combine beans, chilies, corn, ¾ cup cheese, rice, bell peppers, salt, onion powder, cumin, oregano, cayenne pepper, and black pepper. Mix well.

3 Spoon mixture into prepared pan. Place pan inside air fryer.

4 Air fry 15 minutes, then top with remaining ½ cup cheese. Air fry an additional 5 minutes. Serve warm.

PER SERVING

CALORIES: 375 | FAT: 11g | PROTEIN: 19g | SODIUM: 972mg | FIBER: 13g | CARBOHYDRATES: 47g | SUGAR: 4g

Vegetable Garden Pizzas

Air fryer pizza is quick and delicious. It can be customized to fit your tastes with individual toppings. This recipe is made with pesto and a great combination of vegetables. Make sure to follow the steps for covering the pizza with a bowl, as the cheese and toppings tend to want to fly around inside the air fryer.

Hands-On Time: 15 minutes
Cook Time: 10 minutes (per batch)
Total Recipe Cost: $11.61

Serves 4

- ½ (6.7-ounce) jar pesto
- 4 (8") precooked pizza crusts
- 1½ cups mozzarella cheese
- ¼ cup diced broccoli
- ¼ cup sliced black olives
- ¼ cup diced zucchini
- ¼ cup diced white mushrooms
- ½ cup grated Parmesan cheese

1 Preheat air fryer to 400°F.

2 Spread pesto in a thin layer on pizza crusts. Sprinkle mozzarella over pesto.

3 Top each pizza with broccoli, olives, zucchini, and mushrooms. Sprinkle Parmesan on top of each pizza.

4 Carefully place pizzas inside air fryer and cover with an inverted oven-safe bowl. Air fry 7 minutes (you may need to work in batches).

5 Carefully remove bowl (it will be hot) from top of pizzas.

6 Air fry an additional 3 minutes. Serve.

PER SERVING

CALORIES: 653 | FAT: 24g | PROTEIN: 28g | SODIUM: 1,575mg | FIBER: 3g | CARBOHYDRATES: 78g | SUGAR: 3g

Corn Fritters

You are in for a real treat with these slightly sweet and slightly savory Corn Fritters air fried to a crisp perfection! They make a fun and affordable main dish and are great when paired with a fresh green salad.

Hands-On Time: 20 minutes
Cook Time: 12 minutes
Total Recipe Cost: $3.68

Serves 4

2 (15-ounce) cans whole kernel corn, drained
1 cup flour
1½ tablespoons granulated sugar
1 teaspoon baking powder
½ teaspoon salt
¼ teaspoon ground black pepper
2 large eggs, beaten
1 cup shredded sharp Cheddar cheese
¾ cup heavy cream

PREPARING AHEAD OF TIME

Corn Fritters can be made ahead of time and refrigerated up to 3 days. They can be eaten warm or cold. Uncooked Corn Fritters can also be frozen up to 1 month in an airtight container. Transfer uncooked Corn Fritters to the airtight container after freezing for an initial 30 minutes.

1 In a medium bowl, combine corn, flour, sugar, baking powder, salt, and pepper. Stir until corn is evenly coated with flour.

2 Mix in eggs, cheese, and cream. Stir to combine.

3 Arrange ⅓-cup scoops onto a cookie sheet, spaced 1" apart. Freeze 30 minutes.

4 Line bottom of air fryer with foil and fold up sides to create a bowl. Preheat air fryer to 400°F.

5 Spray foil bowl with olive oil spray.

6 Arrange fritters in a single layer, spaced ½" apart, inside air fryer. Air fry 12 minutes.

7 To remove, carefully lift foil up and out of air fryer. Peel off fritters. Serve.

PER SERVING

CALORIES: 538 | FAT: 27g | PROTEIN: 17g | SODIUM: 912mg | FIBER: 4g | CARBOHYDRATES: 52g | SUGAR: 10g

Mediterranean Crustless Quiche

This crustless quiche is a great vegetarian main dish that makes a wonderful dinner. It's packed full of protein-rich eggs along with sun-dried tomatoes, spinach, and kalamata olives for a terrific Mediterranean flavor.

Hands-On Time: 15 minutes
Cook Time: 35 minutes
Total Recipe Cost: $9.87

Serves 4

½ cup chopped sun-dried tomatoes
5 large eggs
½ cup half-and-half
½ cup whole milk
1 cup chopped baby spinach
½ cup diced yellow onion
¼ cup pitted and sliced kalamata olives
2 tablespoons minced garlic
1 teaspoon salt
½ teaspoon ground black pepper
1 cup shredded sharp Cheddar cheese
¼ cup crumbled feta cheese

1   Place sun-dried tomatoes in a small glass bowl. Pour 1 cup boiling water over tomatoes and let sit 5 minutes. Drain water.

2   Preheat air fryer to 320°F. Grease a 7" cake pan and set aside.

3   In a large bowl, whisk together eggs, half-and-half, and milk.

4   Stir in tomatoes, spinach, onion, olives, garlic, salt, and pepper. Then fold in Cheddar and feta.

5   Pour contents into prepared cake pan and place inside air fryer.

6   Air fry 35 minutes until a toothpick inserted in the center of quiche comes out clean. Serve.

PER SERVING

CALORIES: 354 | FAT: 24g | PROTEIN: 20g | SODIUM: 1,216mg | FIBER: 2g | CARBOHYDRATES: 11g | SUGAR: 7g

Vegetarian Enchiladas

Enchiladas are so delicious and versatile. In this recipe, the traditional meat filling is substituted with broccoli, cherry tomatoes, and pinto beans.

Hands-On Time: 20 minutes
Cook Time: 30 minutes
Total Recipe Cost: $5.12

Serves 4

2 tablespoons olive oil
½ cup diced yellow onion
1 cup roughly chopped broccoli florets
¼ cup diced cherry tomatoes
1 tablespoon minced garlic
1 teaspoon salt
½ teaspoon ground cumin
⅛ teaspoon ground cinnamon
1 (15.5-ounce) can pinto beans, drained and rinsed
¾ cup red enchilada sauce, divided
4 (8") flour tortillas
½ cup shredded Monterey jack cheese

1 Heat oil in a medium skillet over medium heat. Add onion and cook, stirring occasionally, 3 minutes.

2 Add broccoli and cook an additional 3 minutes, stirring occasionally.

3 Mix in tomatoes, garlic, salt, cumin, and cinnamon. Cook 1 minute. Remove from heat and fold in pinto beans.

4 Preheat air fryer to 320°F.

5 Spread ¼ cup enchilada sauce in bottom of a 7" cake pan.

6 Fill tortillas with bean mixture and roll tortillas up.

7 Arrange rolled tortillas, seam-side down, in cake pan. They will need to be curved a bit to fit. Pour remaining ½ cup enchilada sauce over tortillas.

8 Cover pan with foil. Place pan inside air fryer. Air fry 20 minutes.

9 Remove foil and sprinkle cheese on top. Air fry an additional 3 minutes. Serve warm.

PER SERVING

CALORIES: 381 | FAT: 13g | PROTEIN: 14g | SODIUM: 1,569mg | FIBER: 3g | CARBOHYDRATES: 49g | SUGAR: 6g

Portobello Mushroom Burgers

Portobello Mushroom Burgers are a great way to enjoy the classic burger flavor without the meat. Portobello mushrooms cook quickly in the air fryer and come out perfectly tender with just the right amount of charring on the outside.

Hands-On Time: 10 minutes
Cook Time: 8 minutes
Total Recipe Cost: $10.27

Serves 4

- 4 large portobello mushrooms, stems removed
- ½ cup balsamic vinegar
- ½ cup extra-virgin olive oil
- 1 teaspoon salt
- 1 teaspoon garlic powder
- ½ teaspoon dried basil
- ½ teaspoon dried parsley
- ¼ teaspoon ground black pepper
- 4 (1-ounce) slices provolone cheese
- 4 hamburger buns
- 4 slices beefsteak tomato
- 2 leaves romaine lettuce, halved
- ¼ medium red onion, peeled and thinly sliced

1 Preheat air fryer to 400°F.

2 Arrange mushrooms in a single layer in a shallow baking dish, top-side down.

3 In a small bowl, whisk together vinegar, oil, salt, garlic powder, basil, parsley, and pepper. Pour mixture over mushrooms and let marinate 20 minutes at room temperature.

4 Spray inside of air fryer with olive oil spray.

5 Place marinated mushrooms inside air fryer in a single layer. Air fry 7 minutes.

6 Top each mushroom with 1 cheese slice. Air fry 1 minute.

7 Place mushrooms on bottoms of hamburger buns. Top with tomato, lettuce, onion, and tops of buns. Serve.

PER SERVING

CALORIES: 377 | FAT: 22g | PROTEIN: 14g | SODIUM: 762mg | FIBER: 3g | CARBOHYDRATES: 30g | SUGAR: 8g

Tostadas

This frugal dinner recipe is easy to make and is ready in just 20 minutes. Pepper jack cheese is used, but Colby jack may be substituted if you want less spicy Tostadas.

Hands-On Time: 15 minutes
Cook Time: 4 minutes (per batch)
Total Recipe Cost: $3.47

Serves 4

½ (15-ounce) can vegetarian salsa-style refried beans
4 (6") flour tortillas
4 (1-ounce) slices pepper jack cheese
½ cup pico de gallo
¼ cup sour cream

1 Preheat air fryer to 400°F.

2 Spread beans on top of each tortilla, leaving ½" around the edge, then place 1 cheese slice on top of each.

3 Working in batches, place 1 tortilla inside air fryer at a time.

4 Air fry 4 minutes.

5 Top each tostada with pico de gallo and sour cream. Serve.

PER SERVING

CALORIES: 269 | FAT: 13g | PROTEIN: 12g | SODIUM: 692mg | FIBER: 3g | CARBOHYDRATES: 25g | SUGAR: 3g

Sweet Potato Hash

Sweet Potato Hash is a delicious and filling vegetarian meal that is packed with nutrients.

Hands-On Time: 15 minutes
Cook Time: 15 minutes
Total Recipe Cost: $3.68

Serves 4

2 large sweet potatoes, peeled and diced
1 medium sweet yellow onion, peeled and diced
2 medium stalks celery, sliced
3 tablespoons olive oil
1 teaspoon salt
1 teaspoon garlic powder
½ teaspoon ground black pepper
2 medium green onions, sliced

1 Preheat air fryer to 400°F.

2 In a large bowl, mix together potatoes, onion, celery, oil, salt, garlic powder, and pepper. Toss until evenly coated.

3 Place inside air fryer.

4 Air fry 15 minutes, shaking or turning halfway through the cooking time.

5 Serve topped with green onions.

PER SERVING

CALORIES: 189 | FAT: 10g | PROTEIN: 3g | SODIUM: 631mg | FIBER: 4g | CARBOHYDRATES: 23g | SUGAR: 7g

Blackberry and Goat Cheese Grilled Cheese Sandwiches

Make yourself a fancy grilled cheese at home! With a combination of goat cheese and cream cheese, these sandwiches come out extra creamy with all of the best adult flavors!

Hands-On Time: 15 minutes
Cook Time: 8 minutes (per batch)
Total Recipe Cost: $11.53

Serves 4

4 teaspoons salted butter
8 (¾"-thick) slices white bread
8 ounces crumbled goat cheese
8 ounces whipped cream cheese
12 ounces blackberries

1 Preheat air fryer to 400°F.

2 Spread butter on one side of each bread slice.

3 In a medium bowl, mix goat cheese and cream cheese.

4 Place blackberries in a separate medium bowl and mash well.

5 Build four sandwiches by spreading cheese mixture on 4 bread slices on unbuttered side. Spread blackberries on remaining 4 bread slices on the unbuttered side. Place bread slices together with cheese and blackberries in the center.

6 Hold sandwiches together with toothpicks and place inside air fryer (you may need to work in batches).

7 Air fry 8 minutes, flipping halfway through the cooking time. Serve

PER SERVING

CALORIES: 591 | FAT: 32g | PROTEIN: 22g | SODIUM: 798mg | FIBER: 6g | CARBOHYDRATES: 48g | SUGAR: 11g

Loaded Nachos

Nachos are a delicious and frugal way to enjoy a meatless meal. Packed with beans, cheese, and vegetables, these Loaded Nachos will satisfy your cravings and your hunger.

Hands-On Time: 15 minutes
Cook Time: 4 minutes
Total Recipe Cost: $11.22

Serves 4

- 4 cups thick tortilla chips, divided
- 1 (15-ounce) can vegetarian salsa-style refried beans, divided
- 2 cups shredded Mexican cheese blend, divided
- ½ (4-ounce) can diced jalapeños
- ½ (3.8-ounce) can sliced black olives, drained
- 1 medium Roma tomato, diced
- 1 medium avocado, peeled, pitted, and diced
- ½ cup sour cream

1 Line bottom of air fryer with foil and fold up sides to create a bowl. Preheat air fryer to 400°F.

2 Add 2 cups tortilla chips to foil bowl and spread ½ can beans over chips. Top with 1 cup cheese. Air fry 2 minutes.

3 Top with remaining 2 cups chips, remaining ½ can beans, and remaining 1 cup cheese. Arrange jalapeños and olives on top. Air fry 2 more minutes.

4 Carefully lift foil up and out of air fryer. Top nachos with tomato, avocado, and sour cream. Serve.

PER SERVING

CALORIES: 545 | FAT: 31g | PROTEIN: 22g | SODIUM: 977mg | FIBER: 9g | CARBOHYDRATES: 38g | SUGAR: 3g

Corn and Black Bean Quesadillas

These quesadillas come out extra crispy in the air fryer. This recipe calls for black beans, but if you prefer pinto beans, they will also work well. You can store any uneaten quesadillas in an airtight container in the refrigerator up to 3 days.

Hands-On Time: 10 minutes
Cook Time: 3 minutes (per batch)
Total Recipe Cost: $5.65

Serves 4

- ½ (16-ounce) can black beans, drained and rinsed
- ½ (15-ounce) can whole kernel corn, drained
- ½ (4-ounce) can diced mild green chilies
- 2 cups shredded Mexican cheese blend
- 4 (8") flour tortillas

WHY THE TOOTHPICKS?

Quesadillas tend to want to open up while cooking in the air fryer. Secure your quesadillas well so the cheese can melt and hold the tortillas together.

1 Preheat air fryer to 390°F.

2 In a medium bowl, combine beans, corn, chilies, and cheese. Mix well.

3 Lay out tortillas. Evenly distribute bean mixture onto each tortilla, arranging it on one side.

4 Fold over tortillas so each one is in a half circle. Hold quesadillas together with three toothpicks.

5 Spray inside of air fryer with olive oil spray.

6 Working in batches, spray quesadillas with olive oil spray and carefully place inside air fryer.

7 Air fry 3 minutes until crispy, flipping halfway through the cooking time. Serve immediately.

PER SERVING

CALORIES: 420 | FAT: 18g | PROTEIN: 21g | SODIUM: 851mg | FIBER: 6g | CARBOHYDRATES: 41g | SUGAR: 4g

General Tso's Cauliflower

General Tso's Cauliflower is a copycat of the popular chicken dish. In this recipe, cauliflower is breaded and served in a delicious sweet and spicy sauce.

Hands-On Time: 20 minutes
Cook Time: 21 minutes
Total Recipe Cost: $9.92

Serves 4

1 cup cornstarch
4 large eggs, beaten
2 cups panko bread crumbs
1½ teaspoons salt
1½ teaspoons garlic powder
1½ teaspoons paprika
½ teaspoon ground black pepper
1 medium head cauliflower, cut into florets
1 tablespoon sesame oil
2 tablespoons minced garlic
1 tablespoon ginger paste
½ cup low-sodium soy sauce
½ cup vegetable broth
⅓ cup rice wine vinegar
¼ cup granulated sugar
2 tablespoons tomato paste
2 medium green onions, sliced

1 Preheat air fryer to 400°F.

2 Place cornstarch in a medium shallow bowl. Place eggs in a second medium shallow bowl. In a third medium shallow bowl, combine bread crumbs, salt, garlic powder, paprika, and pepper.

3 Dredge cauliflower in cornstarch and turn to coat. Next, dip cauliflower in eggs, shaking off any excess. Finally, dip cauliflower in bread crumb mixture, ensuring all sides are coated.

4 Arrange coated cauliflower inside air fryer and coat well with olive oil spray.

5 Air fry 20 minutes, shaking or turning halfway through the cooking time.

6 While cauliflower is cooking, heat oil in a large skillet over medium heat. Mix in garlic and ginger paste and cook, stirring constantly, 1 minute.

7 Whisk in soy sauce, broth, vinegar, sugar, and tomato paste. Bring to a boil. Reduce heat and let simmer 20 minutes until sauce is thickened.

8 Toss cauliflower in sauce and top with green onions. Serve.

PER SERVING

CALORIES: 406 | FAT: 7g | PROTEIN: 14g | SODIUM: 1,747mg | FIBER: 4g | CARBOHYDRATES: 72g | SUGAR: 20g

Pesto Grilled Cheese Sandwiches

An unexpected but amazing flavor combination for grilled cheese is pesto, tomato, provolone cheese, and American cheese. If you don't have Italian bread on hand, regular white or sourdough bread will work just as well.

Hands-On Time: 12 minutes
Cook Time: 8 minutes (per batch)
Total Recipe Cost: $5.10

Serves 4

- 4 teaspoons salted butter
- 8 slices Italian bread
- 4 tablespoons pesto
- 4 (1-ounce) slices provolone cheese
- 4 slices beefsteak tomato
- 4 (1-ounce) slices American cheese

1 Preheat air fryer to 400°F.

2 Spread butter on one side of each bread slice.

3 Build four sandwiches by spreading pesto on the unbuttered side of bread slices. Top 4 bread slices with 1 slice each provolone, tomato, and American cheese on top of pesto. Place remaining 4 bread slices on top (butter-side out).

4 Hold sandwiches together with toothpicks and place inside air fryer (you may need to work in batches).

5 Air fry 8 minutes, flipping halfway through the cooking time. Serve warm.

PER SERVING

CALORIES: 407 | FAT: 21g | PROTEIN: 18g | SODIUM: 1,128mg | FIBER: 2g | CARBOHYDRATES: 34g | SUGAR: 3g

Spicy Cauliflower

Who knew cauliflower was such a great main dish? In this recipe, you will coat cauliflower in a flavorful sauce, including spicy sriracha! Don't skip the foil bowl, or the sauce will be lost to the bottom of the air fryer. If you don't have foil on hand, a 7" cake pan may be used.

Hands-On Time: 10 minutes
Cook Time: 20 minutes
Total Recipe Cost: $4.26

Serves 4

- 1 medium head cauliflower, cut into florets
- 3 tablespoons sesame oil
- 2 tablespoons low-sodium soy sauce
- 1 tablespoon minced garlic
- 2 tablespoons sriracha
- 2 tablespoons rice wine vinegar
- 2 medium green onions, sliced

1 Line bottom of air fryer with foil and fold up sides to create a bowl. Preheat air fryer to 400°F.

2 Place cauliflower in a large bowl.

3 In a small bowl, whisk together oil, soy sauce, garlic, sriracha, and vinegar. Pour sauce over cauliflower and toss to coat.

4 Place cauliflower inside air fryer in foil bowl. Air fry 20 minutes, stirring halfway through the cooking time.

5 Serve topped with green onions.

PER SERVING

CALORIES: 147 | FAT: 10g | PROTEIN: 4g | SODIUM: 412mg | FIBER: 3g | CARBOHYDRATES: 11g | SUGAR: 5g

Fried Ravioli

You've probably never had ravioli like this! Cheese ravioli is air fried to crispy perfection and dipped in marinara for the perfect easy and fun weekday meal. Remember to keep the ravioli frozen in this recipe; otherwise, it may overcook.

Hands-On Time: 12 minutes
Cook Time: 15 minutes (per batch)
Total Recipe Cost: $10.15

Serves 4

2 large eggs, beaten
2 cups panko bread crumbs
1 teaspoon salt
1 teaspoon garlic powder
¼ teaspoon ground black
   pepper
1 (20-ounce) bag frozen
   cheese ravioli
1 cup marinara sauce

1   Preheat air fryer to 350°F.

2   Place eggs in a medium shallow bowl.

3   In a second medium shallow bowl, combine bread crumbs, salt, garlic powder, and pepper.

4   Dip ravioli first in eggs, shaking off any excess, and then in bread crumbs.

5   Spray inside of air fryer with olive oil spray and arrange ravioli inside air fryer in a single layer. Spray ravioli generously with olive oil spray (you may need to work in batches).

6   Air fry 15 minutes until crispy and golden brown.

7   Serve warm with marinara sauce for dipping.

PER SERVING

CALORIES: 442 | FAT: 9g | PROTEIN: 18g | SODIUM: 968mg | FIBER: 3g | CARBOHYDRATES: 73g | SUGAR: 5g

Desserts

Desserts in the air fryer come out amazing! This chapter has lots and lots of delectable cookie recipes along with recipes for Peach Hand Pies, Pineapple Upside-Down Cake, and Chocolate Chunk Brownies. You'll also find recipes for classic deep-fried desserts like Funnel Cakes and Churros!

Peach Hand Pies

Enjoy peach pie at any time of year with this delicious hand pie recipe. This recipe uses peach pie filling instead of fresh peaches because it is less expensive and available year-round.

Hands-On Time: 30 minutes
Cook Time: 15 minutes (per batch)
Total Recipe Cost: $6.34

Serves 8

2 (9") refrigerated unbaked pie crusts, at room temperature
1 (15-ounce) can peach pie filling
1 cup confectioners' sugar
½ teaspoon vanilla extract
¼ cup whole milk

1 Preheat air fryer to 350°F.

2 Using a 5" plate as a template, cut eight 5" rounds in pie crust dough. When you run out of dough, ball it up and roll it out again.

3 Fill the center of each round with 1 heaping tablespoon pie filling.

4 Brush water around edges of each dough round. Fold dough over to form a half circle and use a fork to crimp edges.

5 Use a sharp knife to cut three small slits in the top of each pie.

6 Spray top of each pie with olive oil spray. Arrange pies inside air fryer so they are not touching (you may need to work in batches).

7 Air fry 15 minutes until golden brown.

8 Carefully remove pies and set aside to cool for 10 minutes.

9 While pies are cooling, in a small bowl, whisk together sugar and vanilla. Slowly whisk in milk until a thin icing forms.

10 Use a fork to drizzle icing over hand pies. Serve.

PER SERVING

CALORIES: 450 | FAT: 13g | PROTEIN: 2g | SODIUM: 267mg | FIBER: 1g | CARBOHYDRATES: 78g | SUGAR: 43g

Caramel Apple Hand Pies

Skip the expensive pie at the restaurant and make your own Caramel Apple Hand Pies at home. This recipe uses canned apple pie filling to save money. The caramel syrup takes this dessert to the next level!

Hands-On Time: 30 minutes
Cook Time: 15 minutes (per batch)
Total Recipe Cost: $7.33

Serves 8

2 (9") refrigerated unbaked pie crusts, at room temperature
1 (15-ounce) can apple pie filling
8 tablespoons caramel syrup
1 cup confectioners' sugar
½ teaspoon vanilla extract
¼ cup whole milk

1 Preheat air fryer to 350°F.

2 Using a 5" plate as a template, cut eight 5" rounds in pie crust dough. When you run out of dough, ball it up and roll it out again.

3 Fill the center of each round with 1 heaping tablespoon pie filling and 1 tablespoon caramel syrup.

4 Brush water around edges of each dough round. Fold dough over to form a half circle and use a fork to crimp edges.

5 Use a sharp knife to cut three small slits in the top of each pie.

6 Spray top of each pie with olive oil spray. Arrange pies inside air fryer so they are not touching (you may need to work in batches).

7 Air fry 15 minutes, until golden brown.

8 Carefully remove pies and set aside to cool for 10 minutes.

9 While pies are cooling, in a small bowl, whisk together sugar and vanilla. Slowly whisk in milk until a thin icing forms.

10 Use a fork to drizzle icing over hand pies. Serve.

PER SERVING

CALORIES: 413 | FAT: 13g | PROTEIN: 2g | SODIUM: 334mg |
FIBER: 2g | CARBOHYDRATES: 70g | SUGAR: 20g

Sprinkle Pudding Cookies

These delicious cookies are perfectly moist and flavorful thanks to the secret ingredient: vanilla pudding mix! This recipe makes a large batch (thirty-six cookies) and yet still costs under $6 to make.

Hands-On Time: 25 minutes
Cook Time: 4 minutes (per batch)
Total Recipe Cost: $5.33

Serves 12

1¼ cups unsalted butter, softened
1 cup granulated sugar
¼ cup packed light brown sugar
1 large egg
1 large egg yolk
1 teaspoon vanilla extract
1 (3.5-ounce) packet instant vanilla pudding mix
2¼ cups all-purpose flour
¾ teaspoon baking soda
¼ teaspoon salt
½ cup sprinkles

1 Preheat air fryer to 350°F.

2 In a large mixing bowl, cream together butter, granulated sugar, and brown sugar, about 3 minutes.

3 Mix in egg, egg yolk, and vanilla. Mix until light and fluffy, about 3 minutes.

4 Pour in pudding mix and stir until combined.

5 In a medium bowl, mix together flour, baking soda, and salt until combined.

6 Slowly mix dry mixture into wet mixture. Stir until fully combined, about 3 minutes. Fold in sprinkles.

7 Spray inside of air fryer with olive oil spray.

8 Working in batches, roll thirty-six heaping tablespoons of dough into balls and arrange ½" apart inside air fryer.

9 Air fry 4 minutes.

10 Transfer to a cooling rack to cool for 10 minutes. Serve.

PER SERVING (SERVING SIZE: 3 COOKIES)

CALORIES: 409 | FAT: 20g | PROTEIN: 3g | SODIUM: 190mg | FIBER: 1g | CARBOHYDRATES: 55g | SUGAR: 36g

Peanut Butter Cookies

This is the easiest peanut butter cookie recipe on the planet! With just three ingredients, you will be amazed at how fast you can have a tasty dessert on the table.

Hands-On Time: 10 minutes
Cook Time: 5 minutes (per batch)
Total Recipe Cost: $1.27

Serves 6

1 cup creamy peanut butter
1 cup granulated sugar
1 large egg

FREEZING PEANUT BUTTER COOKIE DOUGH

If you want to prepare this cookie dough ahead of time and freeze it, you totally can! Prepare the cookie dough to the point of putting it in the air fryer, but instead, arrange the dough balls on a cookie sheet, spaced ½" apart, and freeze them 2 hours. Then place frozen cookie dough into a zip-top freezer bag. Freeze them up to 3 months. Frozen cookie dough can go directly into the air fryer and be cooked 6 minutes.

1 Preheat air fryer to 350°F.

2 In a medium bowl, combine peanut butter, sugar, and egg. Mix well.

3 Roll twelve heaping tablespoons of dough into balls. Slightly press each ball down with the tines of a fork to create a crisscross pattern.

4 Spray inside of air fryer with olive oil spray.

5 Arrange dough balls inside air fryer in a single layer, spaced ½" apart (you may need to work in batches).

6 Air fry 5 minutes.

7 Transfer to a cooling rack to cool for 10 minutes. Serve.

PER SERVING (SERVING SIZE: 2 COOKIES)

CALORIES: 397 | FAT: 22g | PROTEIN: 11g | SODIUM: 19mg |
FIBER: 2g | CARBOHYDRATES: 43g | SUGAR: 38g

Red Velvet White Chocolate Chip Cookies

Do you love the flavor of red velvet? Now you can enjoy it in cookie form with this recipe. If you can't find gel food coloring, regular red food coloring will work.

Hands-On Time: 25 minutes
Cook Time: 5 minutes (per batch)
Total Recipe Cost: $6.68

Serves 18

1½ cups all-purpose flour
¼ cup unsweetened cocoa powder
1 teaspoon baking soda
¼ teaspoon salt
½ cup unsalted butter, softened
1 large egg, room temperature
¾ cup packed light brown sugar
¼ cup granulated sugar
1 tablespoon whole milk
2 teaspoons vanilla extract
1 tablespoon red gel food coloring
2 cups white chocolate chips

GEL FOOD COLOR

Gel food color makes a richer-looking red velvet cookie. It is sold in the baking aisle next to the liquid food color.

1 Preheat air fryer to 350°F.

2 In a medium bowl, mix flour, cocoa powder, baking soda, and salt.

3 In the bowl of a stand mixer (or in a large bowl and using a handheld electric mixer), cream butter about 2 minutes on medium speed.

4 Add egg, sugars, milk, and vanilla to creamed butter. Mix on medium until creamy, about 2 minutes.

5 Add dry ingredients to wet ingredients, ⅓ at a time, mixing after each addition until fully combined.

6 Add food coloring and mix until dough is evenly red.

7 Fold in white chocolate chips.

8 Cover bowl of dough with plastic wrap and refrigerate at least 1 hour.

9 Working in batches, roll thirty-six heaping tablespoons of dough into balls and arrange ½" apart inside air fryer.

10 Air fry 5 minutes. Remove cookies from air fryer. While cookies are still warm, gently press down on tops with the bottom of a glass until crinkles form.

11 Transfer to a cooling rack to cool for 10 minutes. Serve.

PER SERVING (SERVING SIZE: 2 COOKIES)

CALORIES: 241 | **FAT:** 11g | **PROTEIN:** 3g | **SODIUM:** 127mg | **FIBER:** 1g | **CARBOHYDRATES:** 32g | **SUGAR:** 23g

Ranger Cookies

Make these tasty Ranger Cookies—a chocolate chip cookie with a delicious crunch thanks to the addition of coconut, rolled oats, and cornflakes! If you've never heard of Ranger cookies, they originated in Texas and were sometimes called "Texas Ranger Cookies" and have now been shortened to "Ranger Cookies."

Hands-On Time: 25 minutes
Cook Time: 5 minutes (per batch)
Total Recipe Cost: $6.68

Serves 24

- 1 cup unsalted butter, softened
- 1 cup granulated sugar
- 1 cup packed light brown sugar
- 1 teaspoon vanilla extract
- 2 large eggs
- 2 cups all-purpose flour
- 1 teaspoon baking soda
- ½ teaspoon baking powder
- ½ teaspoon salt
- 2 cups old-fashioned (rolled) oats
- 2 cups cornflakes
- 1 cup unsweetened coconut flakes
- 8 ounces milk chocolate chips

1 Preheat air fryer to 350°F.

2 In a large bowl and using an electric mixer, cream together butter and sugars until light and fluffy, about 2–3 minutes.

3 Mix in vanilla and then eggs one at a time.

4 In a medium bowl, whisk together flour, baking soda, baking powder, and salt. Add oats and stir well.

5 Add dry ingredients to wet ingredients and mix until combined.

6 Fold in cornflakes, coconut, and chocolate chips.

7 Working in batches, roll forty-eight tablespoons of dough into balls and arrange ½" apart inside air fryer.

8 Air fry 5 minutes.

9 Transfer to a cooling rack to cool for 10 minutes. Serve.

PER SERVING (SERVING SIZE: 2 COOKIES)

CALORIES: 292 | FAT: 13g | PROTEIN: 4g | SODIUM: 145mg | FIBER: 2g | CARBOHYDRATES: 39g | SUGAR: 23g

Salted Caramel Cookies

These Salted Caramel Cookies are thin and crispy and have a sweet caramel flavor and smooth white chocolate chips. The salt dusted on top adds an extra-special pop!

Hands-On Time: 25 minutes
Cook Time: 5 minutes (per batch)
Total Recipe Cost: $6.40

Serves 24

1 cup unsalted butter, softened
½ cup granulated sugar
½ cup packed light brown sugar
1 teaspoon vanilla extract
2 large eggs
½ cup caramel syrup
2¼ cups flour
1 teaspoon baking soda
½ teaspoon salt
2 cups white chocolate chips
1 tablespoon coarse sea salt

1 Preheat air fryer to 350°F.

2 In a large bowl and using an electric mixer, cream together butter and sugars until light and creamy, about 2–3 minutes.

3 Mix in vanilla and then eggs one at a time.

4 Pour in caramel syrup and mix until combined.

5 Add flour, baking soda, and salt to bowl. Give mixture a few stirs before mixing with electric mixer so flour stays in bowl. Mix on low until combined.

6 Fold in white chocolate chips.

7 Working in batches, roll forty-eight table-spoons of dough into balls and arrange ½" apart inside air fryer.

8 Air fry 5 minutes. Remove cookies from air fryer and immediately sprinkle with sea salt.

9 Transfer to a cooling rack to cool for 10 minutes. Serve.

PER SERVING (SERVING SIZE: 2 COOKIES)

CALORIES: 243 | FAT: 12g | PROTEIN: 3g | SODIUM: 385mg | FIBER: 0g | CARBOHYDRATES: 31g | SUGAR: 17g

Funnel Cakes

Make this popular carnival treat at home with your air fryer. A squeezable plastic bottle is used in this recipe, but if you don't have one, you can spoon the batter into a sandwich bag with a small corner cut off.

Hands-On Time: 20 minutes
Cook Time: 3 minutes (per batch)
Total Recipe Cost: $0.82

Serves 4

½ cup whole milk
2 large eggs
1 teaspoon vanilla extract
2 tablespoons granulated sugar
1½ teaspoons baking powder
½ teaspoon salt
1 cup all-purpose flour
¼ cup confectioners' sugar

1 Place a 7" cake pan inside air fryer. Preheat air fryer to 370°F.

2 In a medium bowl, whisk together milk, eggs, and vanilla. Mix until fully combined.

3 Add granulated sugar, baking powder, and salt. Mix to combine.

4 Add flour and mix until smooth.

5 Working in four batches, place batter in a squeezable plastic bottle. Drizzle ¼ of batter in preheated cake pan inside air fryer so it crisscrosses over itself in a lattice pattern.

6 Air fry 3 minutes, flipping halfway through the cooking time.

7 Serve cakes with a dusting of confectioners' sugar.

PER SERVING

CALORIES: 204 | FAT: 3g | PROTEIN: 7g | SODIUM: 522mg | FIBER: 1g | CARBOHYDRATES: 34g | SUGAR: 10g

Churros

Make your own cinnamon-sugar-coated Churros at home with this easy and frugal recipe! Don't skip the step of chilling the dough, or your Churros won't hold their shape inside the air fryer.

Hands-On Time: 15 minutes
Cook Time: 10 minutes (per batch)
Total Recipe Cost: $1.28

Serves 6

¼ cup unsalted butter
½ cup whole milk
½ teaspoon salt
½ cup all-purpose flour
2 large eggs
2 teaspoons vanilla extract
¼ cup granulated sugar
1 teaspoon ground cinnamon

1 Melt butter in a medium skillet over medium-high heat. Whisk in milk and salt.

2 Bring to a boil and immediately lower heat to medium, stirring continuously.

3 Mix in flour and continue to stir until a dough forms, around 1 minute.

4 Remove from heat and let cool 5 minutes.

5 Mix in eggs and vanilla and stir until fully combined. Spoon dough into a pastry bag fitted with a star tip.

6 Pipe dough into six 4"-long logs and transfer to refrigerator to chill 1 hour.

7 In a small bowl, whisk together sugar and cinnamon and then spread on a large shallow plate. Set aside.

8 Preheat air fryer to 340°F. Spray inside of air fryer with olive oil spray.

9 Arrange Churros inside air fryer, spaced 1" apart. Air fry 5 minutes (you may need to work in batches).

10 Remove Churros from air fryer and immediately dip in sugar-cinnamon mixture.

11 Transfer to a cooling rack to cool for 10 minutes. Serve.

PER SERVING

CALORIES: 178 | FAT: 9g | PROTEIN: 4g | SODIUM: 227mg |
FIBER: 1g | CARBOHYDRATES: 18g | SUGAR: 10g

Fried Chocolate Sandwich Cookies

Try this classic carnival treat at home, made for just pennies! These delicious fried cookies taste great on their own or dipped in a glass of cold milk.

Hands-On Time: 20 minutes
Cook Time: 8 minutes (per batch)
Total Recipe Cost: $0.67

Serves 4

1 (8-ounce) can refrigerated crescent roll dough
8 chocolate sandwich cookies
¼ cup confectioners' sugar

FRIED CANDY?

You can also follow this recipe to make your own fried candy! Choose a fun-sized chocolate candy in your favorite flavor (think peanut butter cups, and so on) and wrap it in the dough as directed. Air fry 8 minutes and enjoy.

1 Preheat air fryer to 360°F.

2 Separate dough into eight individual pieces.

3 Place 1 cookie in center of each dough piece. Wrap dough around cookie until completely covered. Pinch edges to seal.

4 Arrange wrapped cookies inside air fryer, spaced 1" apart (you may need to work in batches).

5 Spray tops and sides of wrapped cookies with olive oil spray. Air fry 8 minutes.

6 Remove cookies from air fryer and sprinkle with confectioners' sugar.

7 Transfer to a cooling rack to cool for 10 minutes. Serve.

PER SERVING (SERVING SIZE: 2 COOKIES)

CALORIES: 337 | FAT: 15g | PROTEIN: 5g | SODIUM: 518mg | FIBER: 1g | CARBOHYDRATES: 48g | SUGAR: 22g

Cherry Cobbler

In this recipe, you will use a can of cherry pie filling topped with homemade cobbler topping. The air fryer makes the cobbler topping extra crispy and cooks the dessert in just 10 minutes.

Hands-On Time: 15 minutes
Cook Time: 10 minutes
Total Recipe Cost: $3.84

Serves 4

- 1 (20-ounce) can cherry pie filling
- ¾ cup granulated sugar
- ¾ cup all-purpose flour
- ½ teaspoon salt
- 6 tablespoons unsalted butter, melted
- 1 teaspoon vanilla extract

1 Preheat air fryer to 330°F. Grease a 7" cake pan.

2 Pour pie filling into prepared pan.

3 In a medium bowl, mix together sugar, flour, and salt.

4 Slowly drizzle in melted butter and vanilla. Mix together with a fork until mixture forms pea-sized balls.

5 Grab small handfuls of dough and roll into balls. Flatten rounds and arrange over pie filling, overlapping slightly.

6 Place pan inside air fryer. Air fry 10 minutes until cobbler is golden brown.

7 Transfer to a cooling rack to cool for 30 minutes. Serve.

PER SERVING

CALORIES: 548 | FAT: 16g | PROTEIN: 3g | SODIUM: 318mg | FIBER: 1g | CARBOHYDRATES: 95g | SUGAR: 38g

Chocolate Chunk Brownies

These brownies are a real crowd pleaser! Not only do brownies cook faster in the air fryer, but they also come out extra crispy around the edges!

Hands-On Time: 15 minutes
Cook Time: 15 minutes (per batch)
Total Recipe Cost: $3.89

Serves 6

½ cup unsalted butter, softened
2 cups granulated sugar
2 large eggs
1 teaspoon vanilla extract
½ cup all-purpose flour
⅓ cup unsweetened cocoa powder
¼ teaspoon salt
¼ teaspoon baking powder
1 cup semisweet chocolate chunks

1 Preheat air fryer to 330°F. Grease a 7" cake pan and set aside.

2 In a large bowl, cream together butter and sugar until light and fluffy, about 4 minutes.

3 Mix in eggs one at a time. Mix in vanilla and stir until fully combined.

4 In a medium bowl, whisk together flour, cocoa powder, salt, and baking powder.

5 Working in batches, slowly mix dry ingredients into wet ingredients. Fold in chocolate chunks.

6 Pour brownie batter into prepared pan.

7 Place pan inside air fryer. Air fry 15 minutes until a toothpick inserted in the center of brownies comes out clean.

8 Transfer to a cooling rack to cool for 30 minutes. Serve.

PER SERVING

CALORIES: 613 | FAT: 25g | PROTEIN: 6g | SODIUM: 147mg |
FIBER: 4g | CARBOHYDRATES: 97g | SUGAR: 83g

Pineapple Upside-Down Cake

Pineapple Upside-Down Cake may seem fancy, but it's actually incredibly easy to make. The trick is arranging the pineapple slices and maraschino cherries in a pretty design at the bottom of your cake dish before topping it with cake batter.

Hands-On Time: 20 minutes
Cook Time: 25 minutes
Total Recipe Cost: $7.82

Serves 6

- 1 (8-ounce) can pineapple slices, drained
- 12 maraschino cherries, stems removed
- ⅓ cup packed light brown sugar
- 2 tablespoons unsalted butter, chilled and cut into small chunks
- ½ cup unsalted butter, softened
- 1 cup granulated sugar
- 2 large eggs
- 1 large egg yolk
- 2 teaspoons vanilla extract
- 1½ cups cake flour
- 2 teaspoons baking powder
- ¼ teaspoon salt
- ¾ cup buttermilk

1 Preheat air fryer to 320°F. Grease a 7" cake pan.

2 Arrange pineapple slices in a single layer on bottom of prepared pan, breaking slices in half to fit as needed.

3 Place cherries in openings of pineapple slices in a decorative pattern. Sprinkle with brown sugar and chilled butter. Set aside.

4 In a large mixing bowl, cream together softened butter and granulated sugar. Mix 4 minutes until fluffy.

5 Mix in eggs and egg yolk, one at a time, then mix in vanilla.

6 In a medium bowl, combine flour, baking powder, and salt.

7 Slowly mix flour mixture and buttermilk into wet mixture, alternating between flour and buttermilk until ingredients are fully combined.

8 Pour batter into prepared pan and place inside air fryer.

9 Air fry 25 minutes until a toothpick inserted in the center of cake comes out clean.

10 Run a knife around the edge of pan to loosen cake. Place a serving plate on top of pan and flip pan over onto plate. Keep pan on top of cake for about 5 minutes and then remove and let cake cool for 20 minutes. Serve.

PER SERVING

CALORIES: 557 | FAT: 21g | PROTEIN: 7g | SODIUM: 323mg | FIBER: 1g | CARBOHYDRATES: 83g | SUGAR: 55g

Apple Dumplings

Apple Dumplings are like apple hand pies, but they are cooked in an amazing apple cider sauce that just begs for a scoop of vanilla ice cream. They take a bit longer to cook but still cost less than $5!

Hands-On Time: 20 minutes
Cook Time: 30 minutes
Total Recipe Cost: $4.84

Serves 8

1 (8-ounce) can refrigerated crescent roll dough
2 small Gala apples, cored, peeled, and quartered
8 tablespoons unsalted butter
⅓ cup packed light brown sugar
⅓ cup granulated sugar
1 teaspoon ground cinnamon
¼ teaspoon ground nutmeg
1 cup apple cider
1 teaspoon vanilla extract

1 Preheat air fryer to 330°F.

2 Separate dough into eight individual pieces.

3 Place 1 apple piece in center of each dough piece. Wrap dough around apple until completely covered. Pinch edges to seal. Arrange apple dumplings in a 7" cake pan.

4 In a small sauté pan over medium-high heat, melt butter, 2 minutes.

5 Whisk in brown sugar, granulated sugar, cinnamon, and nutmeg until combined, 1 minute.

6 Pour in cider and whisk until sugar is dissolved, 2 minutes. Mix in vanilla and then remove from heat.

7 Pour sauce over dumplings in pan and turn dumplings to coat.

8 Place pan inside air fryer. Air fry 25 minutes. Serve warm.

PER SERVING

CALORIES: 303 | FAT: 16g | PROTEIN: 2g | SODIUM: 224mg | FIBER: 1g | CARBOHYDRATES: 38g | SUGAR: 27g

Peach Cobbler

Canned peaches are used in this recipe to save money, as fresh peaches tend to be a lot more expensive. Canned peaches also allow for this dish to be made at any time of year instead of just in the summer.

Hands-On Time: 15 minutes
Cook Time: 10 minutes
Total Recipe Cost: $2.49

Serves 4

- 2 (14.5-ounce) cans cling peaches, drained
- ¾ cup plus 3 tablespoons granulated sugar, divided
- 3 tablespoons packed light brown sugar
- 1½ teaspoons vanilla extract, divided
- ½ tablespoon cornstarch
- ½ teaspoon ground cinnamon
- ¾ cup all-purpose flour
- ½ teaspoon salt
- 6 tablespoons unsalted butter, melted

1 Preheat air fryer to 330°F.

2 In a 7" cake pan, add peaches, 3 tablespoons granulated sugar, brown sugar, ½ teaspoon vanilla, cornstarch, and cinnamon. Stir.

3 In a medium bowl, mix together remaining ¾ cup granulated sugar, flour, and salt.

4 Slowly drizzle in melted butter and remaining 1 teaspoon vanilla. Mix together with a fork until mixture forms pea-sized balls.

5 Grab small handfuls of dough and roll into balls. Flatten rounds and arrange over peach filling, overlapping slightly.

6 Place pan inside air fryer. Air fry 10 minutes until cobbler is golden brown.

7 Transfer to a cooling rack to cool for 30 minutes. Serve.

PER SERVING

CALORIES: 606 | FAT: 16g | PROTEIN: 4g | SODIUM: 307mg | FIBER: 3g | CARBOHYDRATES: 112g | SUGAR: 86g

Plum Crisp

Fresh plums topped with a delicious crisp topping make the perfect summer dessert. Rolled oats mixed with brown sugar and cinnamon bring out the flavor of the fruit while still keeping this dessert extremely affordable.

Hands-On Time: 20 minutes
Cook Time: 20 minutes
Total Recipe Cost: $2.56

Serves 6

2 cups chopped plums
½ cup packed light brown sugar, divided
⅛ cup granulated sugar
1½ teaspoons cornstarch
½ cup old-fashioned (rolled) oats
½ cup all-purpose flour
¼ teaspoon ground cinnamon
¼ teaspoon salt
⅛ teaspoon ground nutmeg
⅓ cup unsalted butter, melted

1 Preheat air fryer to 350°F. Grease a 7" cake pan.

2 Place plums, ¼ cup brown sugar, granulated sugar, and cornstarch in prepared pan. Stir until plums are evenly coated.

3 In a medium bowl, whisk together oats, flour, remaining ¼ cup brown sugar, cinnamon, salt, and nutmeg.

4 Slowly pour melted butter into oat mixture and mix with a fork until it turns crumbly.

5 Sprinkle oat mixture over plums.

6 Place pan inside air fryer. Air fry 20 minutes.

7 Transfer to a cooling rack to cool for 20 minutes. Serve.

PER SERVING

CALORIES: 273 | FAT: 10g | PROTEIN: 2g | SODIUM: 103mg | FIBER: 2g | CARBOHYDRATES: 42g | SUGAR: 28g

Apple Crisp

Gala apples are used in this recipe, but any sweet red apple variety may be used. Shop around and choose the most affordable option at your grocery store.

Hands-On Time: 20 minutes
Cook Time: 20 minutes
Total Recipe Cost: $2.97

Serves 6

- 3 small Gala apples, peeled, cored, and sliced
- ¼ cup granulated sugar
- 1 tablespoon lemon juice
- ½ teaspoon ground cinnamon
- ½ cup old-fashioned (rolled) oats
- ½ cup all-purpose flour
- ⅓ cup packed light brown sugar
- ¼ teaspoon salt
- ⅓ cup unsalted butter, melted

CAN YOU USE GRANNY SMITH APPLES?

Granny Smith apples also taste great in a crisp. If you choose to make this recipe with that variety, you will want to increase the granulated sugar to ⅓ cup, as Granny Smith apples tend to be extra tart.

1 Preheat air fryer to 350°F. Grease a 7" cake pan.

2 Place apples, granulated sugar, lemon juice, and cinnamon in prepared pan. Stir until apples are evenly coated.

3 In a medium bowl, whisk together oats, flour, brown sugar, and salt.

4 Slowly pour melted butter into oat mixture and mix with a fork until it turns crumbly.

5 Sprinkle oat mixture over apples.

6 Place pan inside air fryer. Air fry 20 minutes.

7 Transfer to a cooling rack to cool for 20 minutes. Serve.

PER SERVING

CALORIES: 271 | FAT: 10g | PROTEIN: 3g | SODIUM: 101mg | FIBER: 2g | CARBOHYDRATES: 42g | SUGAR: 27g

Strawberry Turnovers

These Strawberry Turnovers are a combination of fresh strawberries and chocolate hazelnut spread wrapped in flaky puff pastry and air fried to crispy perfection. If you have trouble getting the edges of the puff pastry to stick together, add a little bit of water to your fingertips and pinch the edges closed.

Hands-On Time: 20 minutes
Cook Time: 15 minutes
Total Recipe Cost: $7.62

Serves 9

1 (17.3-ounce) box frozen puff pastry sheets, thawed
½ cup chocolate hazelnut spread
9 large strawberries, hulled and quartered
1 large egg yolk
1 tablespoon water

FROZEN STRAWBERRIES?

Frozen strawberries will save you even more money. Make sure to let them defrost for an hour before using, and drain any extra liquid.

1 Preheat air fryer to 350°F. Spray inside of air fryer with olive oil spray.

2 Roll out puff pastry and cut into eighteen equal squares. Spread 1 tablespoon chocolate hazelnut spread in center of each pastry square and top with two strawberry slices.

3 Fold pastry square in half diagonally and seal edges with a fork.

4 In a small bowl, whisk together egg yolk and water. Brush egg wash over each turnover.

5 Arrange turnovers inside air fryer, spaced 1" apart.

6 Air fry 15 minutes until golden brown. Serve warm.

PER SERVING (SERVING SIZE: 2 TURNOVERS)

CALORIES: 404 | FAT: 25g | PROTEIN: 5g | SODIUM: 145mg | FIBER: 2g | CARBOHYDRATES: 37g | SUGAR: 10g

Banana Chocolate Chip Cake

Banana Chocolate Chip Cake is like the fluffier and sweeter cousin of Banana Bread (see recipe in Chapter 2). It's light enough to be enjoyed as a snack but sweet enough to be eaten as a dessert. I love serving this with a warm cup of coffee.

Hands-On Time: 20 minutes
Cook Time: 20 minutes
Total Recipe Cost: $1.97

Serves 6

¼ cup unsalted butter, softened
½ cup granulated sugar
1 large egg
½ teaspoon vanilla extract
1 cup all-purpose flour
¼ teaspoon baking soda
¼ teaspoon salt
¼ cup buttermilk
1 cup mashed bananas
½ cup mini chocolate chips

1 Preheat air fryer to 360°F. Grease a 7" cake pan and set aside.

2 In a large bowl, cream together butter and sugar. Mix in egg and vanilla.

3 In a medium bowl, whisk together flour, baking soda, and salt.

4 Mix dry ingredients into wet ingredients, then add buttermilk. Stir until just combined.

5 Fold in bananas and chocolate chips. Pour batter into prepared pan and place inside air fryer.

6 Air fry 20 minutes until a toothpick inserted in the center of cake comes out clean.

7 Transfer to a cooling rack to cool for 30 minutes. Serve.

PER SERVING

CALORIES: 335 | FAT: 12g | PROTEIN: 5g | SODIUM: 184mg | FIBER: 2g | CARBOHYDRATES: 50g | SUGAR: 29g

Shortbread Cookies

Shortbread Cookies are quick and affordable. They are made with just three ingredients and cook in just 5 minutes.

Hands-On Time: 20 minutes
Cook Time: 5 minutes (per batch)
Total Recipe Cost: $1.24

Serves 6

1 cup all-purpose flour
½ cup unsalted butter, softened
¼ cup confectioners' sugar

1 Preheat air fryer to 350°F.

2 In a large mixing bowl, combine flour, butter, and sugar. Mix well.

3 Roll out dough to ½" thick and cut twelve cookies using a 2"-circle cookie cutter. When you run out of dough, ball it up and roll it out again.

4 Place cookies inside air fryer, spaced 1" apart (you may need to work in batches).

5 Air fry 5 minutes.

6 Transfer to a cooling rack to cool for 10 minutes. Serve.

PER SERVING (SERVING SIZE: 2 COOKIES)

CALORIES: 227 | FAT: 14g | PROTEIN: 2g | SODIUM: 2mg | FIBER: 1g | CARBOHYDRATES: 20g | SUGAR: 4g

Chewy Chocolate Chip Cookies

Chocolate chip cookies are a favorite for many—and for good reason! These Chewy Chocolate Chip Cookies include walnuts to add an extra layer of flavor and texture.

Hands-On Time: 25 minutes
Cook Time: 5 minutes (per batch)
Total Recipe Cost: $6.74

Serves 24

- 2¼ cups all-purpose flour
- 1 teaspoon baking soda
- 1 teaspoon salt
- 1 cup unsalted butter, softened
- ¾ cup granulated sugar
- ¾ cup packed light brown sugar
- 1 teaspoon vanilla extract
- 2 large eggs
- 1½ cups semisweet chocolate chips
- 1 cup chopped walnuts

1 Preheat air fryer to 350°F.

2 In a medium bowl, whisk together flour, baking soda, and salt.

3 In a large bowl, cream together butter and sugars, about 4 minutes. Mix in vanilla and then eggs one at a time.

4 Slowly pour dry ingredients into wet ingredients and mix until fully combined.

5 Fold in chocolate chips and walnuts.

6 Working in batches, scoop forty-eight heaping tablespoons of dough and place inside air fryer, spaced 1" apart.

7 Air fry 5 minutes.

8 Transfer to a cooling rack to cool for 10 minutes. Serve.

PER SERVING (SERVING SIZE: 2 COOKIES)

CALORIES: 250 | FAT: 14g | PROTEIN: 3g | SODIUM: 159mg | FIBER: 1g | CARBOHYDRATES: 30g | SUGAR: 19g

One-Bowl Salted Chocolate Chip Cookies

This one-bowl recipe is a great way to whip up a batch of cookies without dirtying every dish in the house. Make sure to choose a coarse salt for the topping, as regular table salt will not add the right flavor or texture.

Hands-On Time: 20 minutes
Cook Time: 5 minutes (per batch)
Total Recipe Cost: $3.94

Serves 24

- 2¼ cups all-purpose flour
- 1 teaspoon salt
- ½ teaspoon baking soda
- 1 cup unsalted butter, melted
- ¾ cup granulated sugar
- ¾ cup packed light brown sugar
- 2 large eggs
- 1 teaspoon vanilla extract
- ½ cup dark chocolate chips
- ½ cup semisweet chocolate chips
- 1 teaspoon coarse sea salt

1. Preheat air fryer to 350°F

2. In a large bowl, mix together flour, salt, and baking soda.

3. Add in melted butter, sugars, eggs, and vanilla. Mix well.

4. Fold in dark and semisweet chocolate chips.

5. Working in batches, scoop forty-eight heaping tablespoons of dough and place inside air fryer, spaced 1" apart. Air fry 5 minutes.

6. Immediately remove cookies from air fryer and sprinkle with coarse sea salt.

7. Transfer cookies to a cooling rack to cool for 10 minutes. Serve.

PER SERVING (SERVING SIZE: 2 COOKIES)

CALORIES: 206 | FAT: 10g | PROTEIN: 2g | SODIUM: 187mg | FIBER: 1g | CARBOHYDRATES: 27g | SUGAR: 17g

US/Metric Conversion Chart

VOLUME CONVERSIONS

US Volume Measure	Metric Equivalent
⅛ teaspoon	0.5 milliliter
¼ teaspoon	1 milliliter
½ teaspoon	2 milliliters
1 teaspoon	5 milliliters
½ tablespoon	7 milliliters
1 tablespoon (3 teaspoons)	15 milliliters
2 tablespoons (1 fluid ounce)	30 milliliters
¼ cup (4 tablespoons)	60 milliliters
⅓ cup	90 milliliters
½ cup (4 fluid ounces)	125 milliliters
⅔ cup	160 milliliters
¾ cup (6 fluid ounces)	180 milliliters
1 cup (16 tablespoons)	250 milliliters
1 pint (2 cups)	500 milliliters
1 quart (4 cups)	1 liter (about)

WEIGHT CONVERSIONS

US Weight Measure	Metric Equivalent
½ ounce	15 grams
1 ounce	30 grams
2 ounces	60 grams
3 ounces	85 grams
¼ pound (4 ounces)	115 grams
½ pound (8 ounces)	225 grams
¾ pound (12 ounces)	340 grams
1 pound (16 ounces)	454 grams

OVEN TEMPERATURE CONVERSIONS

Degrees Fahrenheit	Degrees Celsius
200 degrees F	95 degrees C
250 degrees F	120 degrees C
275 degrees F	135 degrees C
300 degrees F	150 degrees C
325 degrees F	160 degrees C
350 degrees F	180 degrees C
375 degrees F	190 degrees C
400 degrees F	205 degrees C
425 degrees F	220 degrees C
450 degrees F	230 degrees C

BAKING PAN SIZES

American	Metric
8 x 1½ inch round baking pan	20 x 4 cm cake tin
9 x 1½ inch round baking pan	23 x 3.5 cm cake tin
11 x 7 x 1½ inch baking pan	28 x 18 x 4 cm baking tin
13 x 9 x 2 inch baking pan	30 x 20 x 5 cm baking tin
2 quart rectangular baking dish	30 x 20 x 3 cm baking tin
15 x 10 x 2 inch baking pan	30 x 25 x 2 cm baking tin (Swiss roll tin)
9 inch pie plate	22 x 4 or 23 x 4 cm pie plate
7 or 8 inch springform pan	18 or 20 cm springform or loose bottom cake tin
9 x 5 x 3 inch loaf pan	23 x 13 x 7 cm or 2 lb narrow loaf or pâté tin
1½ quart casserole	1.5 liter casserole
2 quart casserole	2 liter casserole

Index

Note: Page numbers in **bold** indicate recipe category lists.